THREE-MINUTE THEOLOGY

66 SIMPLE LESSONS ON BASIC BIBLE DOCTRINES

DANA L. GOODNOUGH

Copyright © 2015 Dana L. Goodnough.

All rights reserved. No part of this book may be used or reproduced by any means, graphic, electronic, or mechanical, including photocopying, recording, taping or by any information storage retrieval system without the written permission of the author except in the case of brief quotations embodied in critical articles and reviews.

Scriptures taken from the Holy Bible, New International Version®, NIV®. Copyright © 1973, 1978, 1984, 2011 by Biblica, Inc.™ Used by permission of Zondervan. All rights reserved worldwide. www.zondervan.com The "NIV" and "New International Version" are trademarks registered in the United States Patent and Trademark Office by Biblica, Inc.™ All rights reserved.

WestBow Press books may be ordered through booksellers or by contacting:

WestBow Press
A Division of Thomas Nelson & Zondervan
1663 Liberty Drive
Bloomington, IN 47403
www.westbowpress.com
1 (866) 928-1240

Because of the dynamic nature of the Internet, any web addresses or links contained in this book may have changed since publication and may no longer be valid. The views expressed in this work are solely those of the author and do not necessarily reflect the views of the publisher, and the publisher hereby disclaims any responsibility for them.

Any people depicted in stock imagery provided by Thinkstock are models, and such images are being used for illustrative purposes only. Certain stock imagery © Thinkstock.

ISBN: 978-1-4908-9853-7 (sc)
ISBN: 978-1-4908-9854-4 (e)

Print information available on the last page.

WestBow Press rev. date: 11/20/2015

CONTENTS

Preface ix

The Bible—God's Holy Word
   Revelation 3
   Inspiration 5
   Inerrancy 7
   Infallibility 9
   Illumination 11
   Sufficiency 13

The Triune God
   The Trinity 17
   God the Father...19
   God the Son 21
   God the Holy Spirit...................................... 23

God's Amazing Attributes
   God is Self-Existent 27
   God is Immutable 29
   God is Infinite 31
   God is Omniscient 33
   God is Omnipotent.......................................35
   God is Omnipresent 37
   God is Holy 39
   God is Just...41
   God is Good 43
   God is Gracious 45
   God is Faithful 47
   God is Love.. 49

Jesus Christ our Lord
    Jesus' Deity 53
    Jesus' Incarnation 55
    Jesus' Impeccability... 57
    Jesus' Crucifixion 59
    Jesus' Resurrection 61
    Jesus' Return... 63

The Holy Spirit
    The Indwelling Work of the Holy Spirit 67
    The Baptizing Work of the Holy Spirit..................... 69
    The Filling Work of the Holy Spirit...........................71
    The Empowering Work of the Holy Spirit............... 73

The Spirit World
    The Nature of Angels.. 77
    The Ministry of Angels 79
    Satan 81
    Satan's Defeat.. 83
    Demons 85

The Nature of Humanity
    Created in God's Image 89
    Body, Soul, and Spirit...91
    The Fall 93
    Temptation 95
    Sin and the Sin Nature 97

Such a Great Salvation
    Salvation 101
    Atonement..103
    Redemption 105
    Propitiation..107
    Substitution 109

Your Position in Christ
- Justification 113
- Sanctification 115
- Glorification 117
- Regeneration 119
- Reconciliation 121
- Adoption 123

Seven Snapshots of the Local Church
- The Church as a Body 127
- The Church as a Building 129
- The Church as a Bride 131
- The Church as a Family 133
- The Church as a Flock 135
- The Church as a Grapevine 137
- The Church as a Priesthood 139

The Future
- The Rapture 143
- The Resurrection 145
- The Second Coming 147
- Judgment Day 149
- The Millennial Kingdom 151
- Heaven, Hell, and Eternity 153

PREFACE

• • • • • • • •

Theology! The word itself can either intrigue the mind or frighten the faithful who suspect it of unfathomable depths. Theology simply means the study of God. It's a word that's rich in possibilities for those who want to know God and His ways better, including those who want to live in practical conformity to God's will.

Three Minute Theology covers the major doctrines of the Bible in short, bite sized pieces. Written originally to fit the time limits for "Pastor of the Day" radio messages on The Mars' Hill Network in upstate New York, each lesson is brief and readable. In addition, each lesson cites the Bible as its authoritative foundation. It's my desire to elevate God's truth as discovered in God's Word in the minds and hearts of God's people.

I'm grateful for the support of Wayne Taylor, General Manager of The Mars Hill Network, for providing me with the opportunity to communicate these lessons over the air. I'm also grateful for the people of Pittsford Community Church where I serve as pastor, a church that values God's Word and allows me time to write as a part of my ministry. I'm especially grateful for the loving encouragement of my wife, Monica, who has been my companion through Bible college, seminary, and nearly three decades of ministry.

Now, go ahead. Take three minutes and begin your personal journey in theology.

THE BIBLE— GOD'S HOLY WORD

REVELATION

· · · · · · · ·

Take a look around you and you'll be amazed at what you see. Nature is fascinating, from the tiniest seed to the vast expanses of space. Curious minds have for centuries gazed into the observable universe and discovered all kinds of laws, principles, and insights. But there are some things the human mind couldn't possibly begin to discover, particularly things about God and His ways in this world. The telescope and microscope are inadequate tools for observing God. Instead, God must willingly make Himself known to us.

In fact, God has disclosed much about Himself to us through a process we call "revelation." Through His acts of revelation, God has made known to us certain truths that we could in no way discover on our own. For example, we wouldn't know that God is all-powerful unless He told us so. We wouldn't know that He exists as three-in-one without His self-disclosure about His triune nature. We wouldn't know that Jesus is God in the flesh unless God made that truth known to us through revelation. We certainly wouldn't know that our salvation depends on His grace alone and is received by faith in Jesus Christ alone. These are revealed truths, truths that we couldn't discover on our own. Deuteronomy 29:29 says, *"The secret things belong to the Lord our God, but the things revealed belong to us and to our children forever, that we may follow all the words of this law."*

God has revealed Himself in various ways down through the centuries. At times He has spoken through dreams, visions, angelic pronouncements, and even direct, verbal communication to certain individuals. He spoke to Moses at the burning bush. He spoke to Elijah in a gentle whisper.

God's revelation isn't limited, however, to special people at special times. God has revealed Himself to the whole world through His written Word, the Bible. First Corinthians 2:9-10 tells us, *"'No eye has seen, no ear has heard, no mind has conceived what God has prepared for those who love him'—but God has revealed it to us by his Spirit."* Then in verse 13 Paul says, *"This is what we speak, not in words taught us by human wisdom but in words taught by the Spirit, expressing spiritual truths in spiritual words."* God has spoken through His Word. God's Word is His self-disclosure to the world.

Aren't you glad that God has revealed Himself to us? He has revealed Himself in His Word, the Bible. I hope that you'll read your Bible every day in order to get to know God better. In addition, God has revealed Himself through His Son, Jesus Christ. Jesus came to open the door for us to enter into eternal fellowship with God. He died on the cross so that we can live forever with Him in heaven. Why not turn to Jesus today? Put your faith in Him, and allow Him to help you understand God more and more.

INSPIRATION

· · · · · · · ·

If you've ever read one of Shakespeare's sonnets, listened to a violin concerto by Bach, or observed a painting by Rembrandt, you might have thought to yourself, "These men were truly inspired." At the purely human level, inspiration refers to the heightening of personal skills or insights. An inspired artist inspires our minds and hearts. But when it comes to the Bible, inspiration reaches a whole new level.

According to Second Timothy 3:16-17, *"All Scripture is God-breathed and is useful for teaching, rebuking, correcting and training in righteousness, so that the man of God may be thoroughly equipped for every good work."* When we describe the Bible as the inspired Word of God, we mean much more than the idea of human inspiration. The Bible is inspired by God. It is God-breathed. This means that the Bible is the written expression of God's mind and heart. As such, the Bible speaks with authority. It teaches us God's truth, rebukes our selfish attitudes, corrects our sinful acts, and trains us to live righteous lives.

But how did God produce an inspired Bible? Obviously He didn't write it with His own hand. Instead, God used trustworthy authors to accurately pen His thoughts. Second Peter 1:19-21 tells us, *"And we have the word of the prophets made more certain, and you will do well to pay attention to it, as to a light shining in a dark place, until the day dawns and the morning star rises in your hearts. Above all, you must understand that no prophecy of Scripture came about by the prophet's own interpretation. For prophecy never had its origin in the will of man, but men spoke from God as they were carried along by the Holy Spirit."* These verses inform us that God's Holy Spirit carried the human authors along in a process we call inspiration. This process guarded the writings of these human authors from being merely the musings of men. Instead, what they wrote was and is the Word of God. As such, the Bible deserves our attention. After all, it's a light that shines in a dark world. Frankly, we need all the light we can get. That's why God has given us His written, inspired Word.

Because God has given us His Word through the process of inspiration, we can safely conclude that every word in the Bible carries divine authority. Jesus, in Matthew 5:18, said, *"I tell you the truth, until heaven and earth disappear, not the smallest letter, not the least stroke of a pen, will by any means disappear from the Law until everything is fulfilled."* We can trust every word, even every letter, in the Bible to have the mark of God's truth.

It's amazing to realize that God's inspired Word is readily available to each and every one of us today. Why not take your copy of the Bible off the shelf, open it up, and immerse yourself in the mind and heart of God. Then thank its Author for the gift of eternal life that can be yours by putting your faith in Jesus Christ.

INERRANCY

· · · · · · · ·

I don't know about you, but I'm thankful that I have spell-check on my computer. It identifies spelling errors that I might not otherwise recognize. However, I still like to proofread my writing, since there are words that fly under the spell-check radar. For example, when I type in the word "right," as in correct, I might misspell it as "write," as in the act of writing. Spell-check wouldn't pick up on this error. By the way, I just used the word "misspell" and am doubly glad for spell-check!

While we strive for accuracy, there's always room for human error. However, the Bible isn't a human book. It's God's book. Because the Bible is the inspired Word of God, we would expect it to meet a higher standard of accuracy. In fact, we would rightly expect the Bible to be inerrant. Inerrancy refers to the concept that the Bible, because it's the product of divine inspiration, is perfectly accurate and without error in any and every way. The Bible is equally inerrant when it describes God's character, when it relates events in human history, when it touches on facts of nature and science, when it describes spiritual matters, and when it makes predictions for the future.

Psalm 18:30 tells us, *"As for God, his way is perfect; the word of the Lord is flawless."* For the Bible to contain errors would mean that either the Bible isn't God's Word or that God isn't perfect. Hebrews 6:18 declares that *"it is impossible for God to lie."* He couldn't implant error in His inspired Word. Second Timothy 3:16 says that *"all Scripture is God-breathed,"* so we know that the Bible claims to be God's Word. The Bible, therefore, must be free from error.

Of course, there have been numerous attacks on the Bible down through the ages. Many people have tried to undermine the Bible's inerrant quality. Some have accused the Bible of being riddled with contradictions, even though competent Bible scholars have repeatedly defended the consistency of God's Word. Others have attempted to identify historical errors in the Bible, often to find out later that further historical and archaeological discoveries have vindicated the Word of God. Still others have attempted to set aside the Bible in favor of modern scientific theories. But even science, rightly understood, doesn't do away with the Bible's inerrancy.

In John 17:17, Jesus said to God the Father, *"Your word is truth."* The Bible is the Word of God. Therefore, the Bible is perfectly true. It is without error. Because the Bible is inerrant, we can trust it to speak accurately about our lives. When the Bible describes us as having fallen short of God's holiness and needing a Savior, we should take notice. When it says that Jesus is that Savior, the only way to forgiveness and peace with God, we should embrace its message. Invite Jesus to be your Savior today, and begin to explore God's inerrant Word. You'll find that you won't be disappointed.

INFALLIBILITY

· · · · · · · ·

Have you ever heard an angry child yell at a parent, "You can't tell me what to do. You're not the boss of me!" In fact, parents do have authority in the home. They can and should tell their children how to behave and what's expected of them. But who's our boss? Who has the authority to tell us how to run our lives? The answer, of course, is that the One who made us has authority over us. God is our boss.

But how can we know with certainty what God wants us to do? Thankfully, God has communicated His love and His expectations to us through His written Word, the Bible. The Bible is the inspired, inerrant Word of God. As such, the Bible speaks with authority.

We sometimes say that the Bible is infallible. Infallibility means much more than that the Bible is without error. It means that the Bible speaks with absolute, divine authority. We can trust that the Bible is true. We must submit ourselves to its precepts, and we can bask in its promises.

In John 10:35 Jesus said, *"The Scripture cannot be broken."* It carries the authority of its divine author. God's purposes cannot be thwarted. His sovereign will must be fulfilled. Therefore, His Word is infallible.

In Jeremiah 23:29 God declares, *"Is not my word like fire, and like a hammer that breaks a rock in pieces?"* These images indicate that we must take seriously the Bible's authority over our lives. In Isaiah 55:11 God says,

"So is my word that goes out from my mouth: It will not return to me empty, but will accomplish what I desire and achieve the purpose for which I sent it." God speaks with authority. His Word is infallible. It will accomplish its appointed purpose.

Because the Bible has authority over our lives, we should eagerly obey its teachings. Jesus, in Matthew 7:24, tells us, *"Therefore everyone who hears these words of mine and puts them into practice is like a wise man who built his house on the rock."* When we build our lives on the solid, authoritative truth of God's Word, our lives will not be devastated by life's storms. James 1:22 states bluntly, *"Do not merely listen to the word, and so deceive yourselves. Do what it says."* Psalm 119:2 reminds us, *"Blessed are they who keep his statutes and seek him with all their heart."*

I'm glad that God has revealed His will to us in His Word. His commands aren't optional, nor are His promises unreliable. He has promised in His Word to grant eternal life to all who believe in Jesus Christ. Have you accepted Jesus as your Savior? Are you living in the blessings of God's Word? Let me invite you to receive Jesus into your heart today, and then begin growing in your faith by reading and responding to God's infallible Word, the Bible.

ILLUMINATION

· · · · · · · ·

If you've ever read a detailed legal document or tried to assemble an appliance based on cryptic instructions, you've probably wished that someone could come alongside you and provide a clear explanation. This sometimes happens when we read the Bible as well. Some passages are difficult to understand. More specifically, some passages are hard to apply in our day to day lives. Just how do we go about loving our neighbor as ourselves? How are we to shine as lights in a dark world? How are we to nurture our children in the faith, or grow in God's grace? Thankfully, we have help in both understanding and applying the truths of God's Word.

First Corinthians 2:12 tells us, *"We have not received the spirit of the world but the Spirit who is from God, that we may understand what God has freely given us."* God the Holy Spirit is our source of spiritual illumination. Illumination refers to the work of God's Holy Spirit whereby He applies the truths of God's Word to our hearts and lives.

We know that the Holy Spirit is active even in the hearts of unbelievers. In John 16:8 Jesus said that the Holy Spirit *"will convict the world of guilt in regard to sin and righteousness and judgment."* The Holy Spirit convicts the hearts of unbelievers, heightening their sense of guilt before God. When we put our faith in Jesus Christ for our salvation, the Holy Spirit takes on a special role in our lives. In 1 Corinthians 3:16 the apostle Paul asks,

"Don't you know that you yourselves are God's temple and that God's Spirit lives in you?" As believers, we have the Holy Spirit living within us. Because of this intimate relationship with God in our lives, we have help in understanding and applying God's Word. The indwelling Holy Spirit illuminates the Bible so that we can live according to its truths.

The Holy Spirit's work of illumination, however, doesn't take away our need to read and study the Bible. Second Timothy 2:15 tells us, *"Do your best to present yourself to God as one approved, a workman who does not need to be ashamed and who correctly handles the word of truth."* Studying the Bible demands hard work. We shouldn't expect the Holy Spirit to allow us to bypass the work involved in studying and meditating on God's Word. We'd miss out on the joy of discovering what God has to say to us each day. But we can depend on the Holy Spirit to take those truths that we've studied and apply them to our own situation. He, through His gentle and often mysterious leading in our hearts, will help us weave God's Word into our daily lives.

The illuminating work of the Holy Spirit is available to every true believer. God wants us to understand His Word and use it effectively. First, however, we must establish a relationship with God through faith in Jesus Christ. Ask Jesus to be your Savior today, and then invite the Holy Spirit to open your heart so that you can live according to God's Word.

SUFFICIENCY

· · · · · · · ·

I'll be the first to admit that I often wish God had given us more information about almost every topic. I wish I knew more about heaven, about creation, about the spirit world, about our human makeup, about God Himself, about ... well, about everything! But God has given us all that we need to know about Him and His purposes in the Bible. We can say that the Bible is sufficient.

Second Peter 1:3-4 tells us, *"His divine power has given us everything we need for life and godliness through our knowledge of him who called us by his own glory and goodness. Through these he has given us his very great and precious promises, so that through them you may participate in the divine nature and escape the corruption in the world caused by evil desires."* God has given us everything we need to live spiritual lives. He has revealed these great and precious promises in His Word.

The sufficiency of the Bible teaches us that the Word of God has the answers to life's most puzzling questions. Granted, the Bible won't necessarily answer our questions in specific ways. For example, we may wonder why God has allowed a close family member to suffer an illness or why we're experiencing a personal financial setback. We may never know the complete answer, but God's Word reveals all that we need to know for now. The Bible tells us that trials build faith and character. James 1:2-3 says, *"Consider it pure joy, my brothers, whenever you face trials of many kinds, because you know that the testing of your faith develops perseverance."* When I go through personal trials, I can be confident that God is at work in my life. He's promised this in the Bible. Therefore, the Bible is sufficient for my need.

Because the Bible is sufficient for my spiritual life, I shouldn't attempt to add to its content. Revelation 22:18-19 warns that we should not add anything or take away any words from that particular book, hinting that there is no need for further revelation about God's plan for His universe. It would be wrong for us to claim to have greater knowledge about such things than the Bible.

Of course, the doctrine of the sufficiency of the Bible doesn't mean that we shouldn't pursue other lines of study. God has created us as thinking, inquisitive beings. We should study God's universe and learn its intricate laws. We should study the human body, mind, and soul in our quest to offer help to hurting people. But when it comes to knowledge about God, the Bible is our only reliable and sufficient source of truth.

The Bible points us to Jesus Christ. He alone is our path to eternal life. To suggest other ways to God is to step beyond the bounds of Scripture. Rather than inventing our own path, why not take the Bible at its word? Turn to Jesus Christ for His free gift of salvation, and then take time to study the Bible for all it's worth. You won't be disappointed.

THE TRIUNE GOD

THE TRINITY

· · · · · · · · ·

There's something appealing about the mysterious. The mystery of life fascinates our minds. The mysteries related to the universe around us, such as black holes or the forces of gravity, magnetism, and light stretch our imaginations. The greatest mystery of all involves the nature of God. God exists in trinity. The Bible reveals this mystery of the triune nature of God.

The word "trinity" means tri-unity, that is, three in one. There is only one true and living God. Deuteronomy 6:4 settles that question. *"Hear, O Israel: The Lord our God, the Lord is one."* Jesus affirmed this truth by quoting this verse in Mark 12:29. Likewise, the New Testament clearly supports the fact that God is one. Romans 3:30 states, *"There is only one God,"* and 1 Timothy 1:17 says, *"Now to the King eternal, immortal, invisible, the only God, be honor and glory for ever and ever."*

While we know that there is only one true God, the Bible also refers to three distinct persons as God—the Father, the Son, and the Holy Spirit. First Corinthians 8:6 identifies the Father as God, saying, *"For us there is but one God, the Father, from whom all things come and for whom we live."* We also learn that the Son, Jesus Christ, is God as stated in Titus 2:13: *"We wait for the blessed hope—the glorious appearing of our great God and Savior, Jesus Christ."* Acts 5:3-4 indicates that the Holy Spirit is God, saying first that Ananias had *"lied to the Holy Spirit"* and then saying that he had lied to God.

Three-Minute Theology

The Father, the Son, and the Holy Spirit are each declared to be God. Yet these three persons are distinct from one another. In Matthew 28:19 Jesus instructed His followers to baptize new believers in the one, unified name of the triune God. He commanded, *"Therefore go and make disciples of all nations, baptizing them in the name of the Father and of the Son and of the Holy Spirit."*

Because God is one and because three distinct persons are called God, we can only conclude that God exists in triunity. The doctrine of the trinity is admittedly beyond our comprehension. It's a mystery of the faith. Furthermore, there's nothing like it in the observable universe, so all illustrations of the trinity fail at some level. However, we can conceive of unity in plurality. Light possesses properties of both particles and energy waves. In math, while one plus one plus one equals three, one times one times one equals one. In marriage, two become one.

Ultimately, we should be pleased to realize that our God is so great that He defies our comprehension. Wouldn't it be disappointing to worship a God who can fit within our limited categories and concepts? Instead, we worship an awesome God who exists as three in one.

GOD THE FATHER

· · · · · · · ·

To say that relationships are important is a gross understatement. God created us to live in relationship with one another and with Him. We value our families. We honor our godly fathers and mothers. We cherish our spouses. We love our children. We're wired for relationships.

God created us to be relationship oriented because He, too, is a relational God. He has existed in relationship forever, the relationship that exists within His triune nature—Father, Son, and Holy Spirit. These three persons are co-equal, co-eternal, and one in essence, yet distinct.

The Bible describes God the Father as having a functional headship within the Trinity. First Corinthians 11:3 says, *"Now I want you to realize that the head of every man is Christ . . . and the head of Christ is God."* Jesus Christ is designated the Son of God, not in the sense that Jesus came into existence at some point in time but in the sense that He shares the same nature as God the Father. This relationship is sometimes called eternal generation. John 3:16 describes Jesus as God's *"only begotten Son."* Likewise, the Holy Spirit exists in a functional relationship with God the Father. That relationship is called eternal procession. In John 15:26 Jesus said, *"When the Counselor comes, whom I will send to you from the Father, the Spirit of truth who goes out from the Father, he will testify about me."* The Holy Spirit goes out from the Father or proceeds from the Father.

God the Father possesses functional headship within the Trinity. According to 1 John 4:14, *"the Father has sent his Son,"* and John 14:16 says that the Father would *"give"* us the Holy Spirit. The Father directs the activities within the triune godhead.

As the Father within the Trinity, God the Father also has a relational role in our lives. Over and over again the Bible describes God in relational terms, referring to Him as our heavenly Father and to us as His children. God loves us dearly. He cherishes us as His own sons and daughters. Of course, our relationship with God the Father is different from that of the Father's relationship with God the Son. But our relationship with God the Father is possible only through God the Son. Jesus came into this world to reveal the Father to us. In John 14:9 Jesus told His disciples, *"Anyone who has seen me has seen the Father."* Jesus also came to restore us to a right relationship with the Father. First John 2:23 tells us, *"Whoever acknowledges the Son has the Father also."*

When we receive Jesus into our hearts by faith we have the privilege, according to Romans 8:15, to call on God as *"Abba, Father."* Take time today to thank God—Father, Son, and Holy Spirit—for this wonderful relationship.

GOD THE SON

· · · · · · · ·

People flock to celebrities. They admire those who are constantly in the spotlight—actors, entertainers, athletes. Some celebrities prove to be men and women of character, but far too many let fame go to their heads. Their lifestyles don't deserve to be celebrated. However, one man stands head and shoulders above all the famous people throughout all human history. This man, Jesus, is far more than a celebrity. In fact, He's far more than a mere man. He's God in the flesh, our Savior and our Lord.

In order to understand who Jesus really is, we must begin with His deity. Jesus is eternal God, one with the Father and the Holy Spirit. In John 10:30 Jesus said, *"I and the Father are one."* Jesus claimed to be God. The apostle Paul confirmed this claim in Titus 2:13 where he wrote that we are waiting for *"the glorious appearing of our great God and Savior, Jesus Christ."* Jesus is God. He's existed from eternity past. He created the universe. Colossians 1:16 says, *"For by him all things were created: things in heaven and on earth, visible and invisible."* Jesus was no ordinary man. He is God.

In addition to His deity, Jesus' unique humanity sets Him apart from all others. Jesus became a human being in a miraculous and mysterious act called the incarnation. John 1:14 tells us, *"The Word,"* that is, the divine Son of God, *"became flesh and made his dwelling among us."* Jesus became a man in time and space. He lived among us.

He worked and ate and slept. He experienced the fullness of human existence. During His earthly life Jesus healed the sick and helped the needy. He taught hungry hearts and pointed us to real, eternal life.

Jesus is God who became a man. But as a man Jesus never sinned, not once. He was the perfect human and therefore became the perfect sacrifice for our sins. Hebrews 4:15 reminds us, *"For we do not have a high priest who is unable to sympathize with our weaknesses, but we have one who has been tempted in every way, just as we are—yet was without sin."* Jesus is the sinless Savior, God in the flesh.

As our sinless Savior, Jesus took our sins on Himself when He died on the cross. *"He is the atoning sacrifice for our sins,"* as 1 John 2:2 says. Jesus died for our sins on the cross, but He rose from the dead to give us life. Those who trust in Jesus receive His free gift of eternal life. That's why Jesus stands out in our world. That's why Jesus stands out in our hearts. Why not commit your heart to Jesus today? He's eager to share His life with you.

GOD THE HOLY SPIRIT

· · · · · · · ·

God is one. Yet God exists in trinity, a tri-unity of Father, Son, and Holy Spirit. Of the three persons in the godhead, the Holy Spirit is perhaps the most mysterious to our minds. We can conceptualize God the Father to some degree. God the Son, because of the incarnation, is much more understandable to us. But God the Holy Spirit? By nature a spirit being is intangible, elusive, and mysterious. However, the Bible reveals that God the Holy Spirit is real, personal, and powerful. He's active in the world today and He's personally active in our lives.

In order to understand how the Holy Spirit works among us, we must first recognize that He possesses personality. That is to say, the Holy Spirit exhibits intellect, emotion, and will. First Corinthians 2:10 says, *"The Spirit searches all things, even the deep things of God."* The Holy Spirit has intellect. In fact, He's all-knowing. The Holy Spirit also possesses emotion. He can be grieved, according to Ephesians 4:30. Romans 15:30 refers to the *"love of the Spirit."* The Holy Spirit both thinks and feels. He also acts—He has a will. He *"determines,"* according to 1 Corinthians 12:11, how He will distribute spiritual gifts within the body of Christ. The Holy Spirit, therefore, isn't some impersonal force. He possesses personality. He thinks, feels, and acts.

We must also realize that the Holy Spirit is a superior person, one with the Father and the Son, sharing equally the attributes of deity within the triune godhead. For example, the Holy Spirit is omnipresent. Psalm 139:7-8 says, *"Where can I go from your Spirit? Where can I flee from your presence? If I go up to the heavens, you are there; if I make my bed in the depths, you are there."* The Holy Spirit is also omnipotent. He can create life. Job 33:4 reminds us, *"The Spirit of God has made me,"* and Romans 8:11 says that the Spirit *"raised Jesus from the dead."* The Holy Spirit is God.

The Holy Spirit is active in our world today. John 16:8 says that the Holy Spirit convicts the world of guilt in regard to sin. Titus 3:5 tells us, *"He saved us through the washing of rebirth and renewal through the Holy Spirit."* Conviction, regeneration, and empowering for service are all works of the Holy Spirit of God. One important part of the Holy Spirit's work is revealed in John 16:14. Jesus said, *"He will bring glory to me by taking from what is mine and making it known to you."* In many ways the Holy Spirit is the behind-the-scenes member of the trinity. He delights in pointing people to Jesus Christ. Have you received Jesus Christ as your Savior? Why not follow the Spirit's prompting and give yourself to Christ today?

GOD'S AMAZING ATTRIBUTES

GOD IS SELF-EXISTENT

· · · · · · · ·

Where did God come from? This was a question I remember asking as a child. Although this is an innocent and childlike question, the nature of the existence of God puzzles even the greatest minds. After all, everything we see around us had a beginning. We celebrate a birthday because that's the day we entered into this world. We mark buildings with a date chiseled into the cornerstone to remember when that building was erected. Even the universe had a beginning, though people debate how long ago that took place. But what about God? Where did He come from?

The Bible describes God as self-existent. He didn't have a beginning. No one created Him. God is without origin, the uncaused cause. He exists all on His own. We could say that God not only gives life, but that He is life itself.

When God revealed Himself to Moses at the burning bush, He declared His special, personal name. According to Exodus 3:14, God said, *"I AM who I AM. This is what you are to say to the Israelites: 'I AM has sent me to you.'"* God describes Himself as "I AM," implying that God is living and exists in and of Himself. The name "I AM" has come down to us from Hebrew roughly as the name "Jehovah" or "Yahweh." Moses didn't need to fear God's will because God is a living, self-existing being. Since no one else can make such a claim, we know that no one else is more powerful than God. We can trust Him because He exists independently from His creation. He doesn't depend on us, but we must depend on Him.

It's interesting to discover that, in the New Testament, Jesus underscored the self-existence of God the Father and claimed equality with God's self-existent nature. In John 5:26 Jesus said, *"For as the Father has life in himself, so he has granted the Son to have life in himself."* God the Father is self-existent, and God the Son shares in that divine, self-existent nature. Jesus frequently used the personal name of God to describe Himself. He claimed to be the "I AM" of the burning bush. Jesus described Himself by saying *"I am the bread if life," "I am the light of the world," "I am the good shepherd,"* and *"I am the resurrection and the life."* These and similar claims identify Jesus as God in the flesh, the self-existent God.

Since God exists all on His own, doesn't it make sense that we can trust Him to take care of us? Although God doesn't depend on us for His existence, we depend on Him. Furthermore, since Jesus is the self-existent God in the flesh, what better step could we take than to entrust our lives to Him? He wants to change our lives and He offers us eternal life. Why not turn to Jesus for life today?

GOD IS IMMUTABLE

· · · · · · · ·

Someone said that the only thing in life that's consistent is change. How true! Our children change, growing up and going out faster than we can imagine. Our bodies change with age. Styles change. Technology changes constantly. The computer you buy today is obsolete tomorrow. Whole nations change. While change is often beneficial, sometimes change is destructive. The rust on your car or the broken pipe in your basement is a testimony to destructive change. Our society's slide into immorality is a change that's troubling to many Christians and non-Christians alike.

With change everywhere around us, we need something—someone on whom we can depend. That someone is God. While God's creation is changing, God Himself never changes. He is immutable. Think about it for a moment. If God were to change, He'd either have to become better or worse. Since God is perfect, He cannot change for the worse, nor can He change for the better. He's already perfect. Therefore, God by His very nature cannot change.

The immutability of God is a source of comfort to us in our changing world. Just try to imagine what life would be like if God were fickle, constantly changing in nature. One day He might be loving and the next day He could be cruel. He might honor honesty today and lying tomorrow.

Who could depend on a God whose nature is constantly in flux? But the God of the Bible is unchanging. In contrast to this changing world, Psalm 102:27 says of God, *"But you remain the same, and your years will never end."* In Malachi 3:6, God declared, *"I the Lord do not change."* According to James 1:17, *"Every good and perfect gift is from above, coming down from the Father of the heavenly lights, who does not change like shifting shadows."*

Aren't you glad that God doesn't change? He always loves us, even when we fail to see His love in the middle of our difficult circumstances. He's faithful even when we're unfaithful. He keeps His promises, including His promise to save all who call on the name of His Son, Jesus Christ. In fact, Jesus Christ, because He's God, is immutable. Hebrews 13:8 states, *"Jesus Christ is the same yesterday and today and forever."* He never changes. He always accepts those who accept Him by faith. He always forgives our sins when we confess them to Him.

In the middle of an unpredictable, changing world, why not put your faith in the unchanging, immutable, faithful God of the Bible? Invite Jesus Christ into your heart today, and keep trusting Him. He will never let you down.

GOD IS INFINITE

· · · · · · · ·

I once had a grade school teacher who would often say, "All good things must come to an end." He offered this bit of proverbial wisdom at the end of recess or a birthday celebration in class. What this teacher was actually saying is that we are limited in what we can do. We have speed limits because driving recklessly would endanger our lives. Our patience is limited, and we sometimes blow up at the people around us. Time is limited. We can only accomplish so much in a day or in a lifetime. I'll admit that many times I wish I had just one more hour in the day, or one more day in the week—especially during a week of vacation! But all good things must come to an end, or so I've heard.

Even though we're limited in time, energy, and even patience, we know that God is not limited. He's infinite. When we say that God is infinite we simply mean that He's unlimited in His character and His attributes. In fact, while we sometimes list ten or twenty attributes of God, such as His holiness, goodness, and love, we would gain a better appreciation for God if we consider the number of His attributes to be limitless. We'll have all eternity to learn more and more about God, and even eternity will not be long enough to exhaust our understanding of the richness of His being. God is infinite.

Furthermore, when it comes to the other attributes of God we find that even these are unlimited. God is unlimited when it comes to time. He is eternal—He had no beginning, He will have no end, and He is outside time itself. Psalm 90:2 declares, *"From everlasting to everlasting you are God."* Since God is eternal, He has time for you. God is also infinite in wisdom. In Romans 11:33, Paul exclaimed, *"Oh the depth of the riches of the wisdom and knowledge of God! How unsearchable his judgments, and his paths beyond tracing out!"* God knows what's best in every situation because His wisdom is infinite. God is also infinite in His love for us. Psalm 36:5 expresses it like this: *"Your love, O Lord, reaches to the heavens, your faithfulness to the skies."* Because God's love for us is unlimited, He never stops loving us. No matter how far from God you may have wandered, He is still ready to welcome you back with open arms. In addition, God is unlimited in power. Jeremiah 32:17 says, *"Ah, Sovereign Lord, you have made the heavens and the earth by your great power and outstretched arm. Nothing is too hard for you."* Is there something in your life today that needs God's unlimited power? Are you facing problems that are way too big for you? They're not too big for God. Nothing is too hard for Him.

Since God is infinite—unlimited in the number and quality of His attributes—don't you think it makes sense to put your trust in Him? Why not ask Jesus, God's Son, to come into your heart today and help you experience the infinite power of God.

GOD IS OMNISCIENT

Nobody likes a know-it-all. You know the kind of person I mean. It's the inexperienced worker who tells you how to do your job better. It's the mom who constantly gives you advice on parenting even though her son is living a worldly lifestyle. It's the man looking over your shoulder telling you how he'd cook the steaks on the grill. People like that are simply annoying. They infer by their comments that they know everything about everything, when in reality they know very little about anything meaningful or important.

When we say that God knows everything, we certainly don't think of Him as a know-it-all. That's because He really does know everything about everything. He is omniscient. By His very nature He possesses unlimited knowledge and wisdom. Psalm 147:5 tells us, *"Great is our Lord and mighty in power; his understanding has no limit."* Job 37:16 says that God is *"perfect in knowledge."* Hebrews 4:13 reminds us, *"Nothing in all creation is hidden from God's sight. Everything is uncovered and laid bare before the eyes of him to whom we must give account."*

The omniscient nature of God is both a source of comfort and challenge to us. It's comforting to realize that God knows everything about my circumstances. He knows my fears, my hurts, my longings, and my hopes.

But God also knows the darkness of my heart. He knows my impure thoughts. He knows my misplaced motives. He sees every act of indiscretion I make. I am accountable to God for everything I do, everything I say, and even everything I think. He knows it all.

Because God's knowledge is unlimited, He even knows the potential outcome of circumstances that never came to be. For example, Jesus, in Matthew 11:21, announced judgment on the cities of Korazin and Bethsaida, saying, *"If the miracles that were performed in you had been performed in Tyre and Sidon, they would have repented long ago."* Jesus, in His omniscience, knew how these ancient cities would have responded had they witnessed His mighty miracles. Not only does God know all things potential, but He knows all things past, present, and future. God, in Isaiah 46:10, declared, *"I make known the end from the beginning, from ancient times, what is still to come."*

Because God knows everything, He knows your needs today. He knows that our greatest need is for our sins to be forgiven. That's why God, before time began, prepared a plan for our salvation. He planned for His Son, Jesus, to die for us. Ephesians 1:4 tells us, *"He chose us in him before the creation of the world."* Why not put your life in the hands of the God who knows you inside and out? Ask Jesus into your life today.

GOD IS OMNIPOTENT

· · · · · · · ·

The most powerful energy source in our solar system is, of course, the sun. Scientists tell us that the sun generates enough energy every second to meet our energy demands on earth for a whole year. That's power! However, even the sun's energy is limited. By contrast, the God who made the sun is unlimited in power. He is omnipotent.

To describe God as omnipotent, or all powerful, is to remember that God is over this universe and still in control of His creation. He isn't weakened by time, and His energy is never depleted. In addition, God has authority over our lives.

Frequently the Bible refers to God as "The Almighty." For example, Revelation 4:8 describes the angels around the throne of God crying out, *"Holy, holy, holy is the Lord God Almighty."* Because God is omnipotent, nothing is too difficult for Him. Jeremiah 32:17 declares, *"Ah, Sovereign Lord, you have made the heavens and the earth by your great power and outstretched arm. Nothing is too hard for you."* Jesus expressed this same idea in Matthew 19:26, saying, *"With God all things are possible."*

Do you realize that your most difficult problem is no problem for God? He's all powerful. He can meet your greatest need. He has already extended His mighty hand of grace and mercy to provide forgiveness for our sins. He did this through His Son, Jesus Christ, who died on the cross to pay our eternal penalty for sin. God is powerful enough to save us, and He's powerful enough to help us overcome life's most demanding difficulties. But we must put our faith in Him. Jesus reminded us in John 15:5, *"Apart from me you can do nothing."* Are you ready to give up trying to solve your own problems and turn to Jesus Christ?

God's all-powerful nature is evident all around us. Creation itself testifies to His power, as Romans 1:20 tells us. *"For since the creation of the world God's invisible qualities—his eternal power and divine nature—have been clearly seen, being understood from what has been made, so that men are without excuse."* We have no reason for doubting God's omnipotence. We can simply look around us and we'll see the evidence of His unlimited power. We can also look at Jesus to see the power of God. It was by God's unlimited power that He raised Jesus from the dead. First Corinthians 6:14 says, *"By his power God raised the Lord from the dead, and he will raise us also."* God has power to create, to save, and to give life. No problem you face will ever tax His power. Nothing is too difficult for Him.

Why not renew your confidence in the unlimited power of God? Thank Him for being all-powerful, and invite Him to work powerfully in your life today.

GOD IS OMNIPRESENT

· · · · · · · ·

God is everywhere. As Christians, we realize that we can see God at work in our daily lives. We can sense the presence of God when we're going through difficult days. We're impressed with the reality of God in our world when we look at His handiwork in creation. God is everywhere around us, and He, through His Holy Spirit, even lives in us by faith.

However, to say that God is everywhere, or omnipresent, isn't the same as pantheism. Pantheism says that God actually *is* everything. He's in the rocks, the trees, the soil, the animals around us—God's existence is inseparably linked with the physical creation. But the Christian concept of God's omnipresence says that His existence is independent of His creation.

King Solomon, in 1 Kings 8:27, declared, *"But will God really dwell on earth? The heavens, even the highest heaven, cannot contain you."* God isn't limited by space. In fact, the entire universe couldn't possibly contain God. Although creation can't contain God, God is present throughout His creation. David wrote in Psalm 139:7-10, *"Where can I go from your Spirit? Where can I flee from your presence? If I go up to the heavens, you are there; if I make my bed in the depths you are there. If I rise on the wings of the dawn, if I settle on the far side of the sea, even there your hand will guide me, your right hand will hold me fast."* David acknowledged the omnipresence of God and took great comfort in knowing that God was present in his life.

While God is equally present everywhere, He hasn't chosen to reveal His presence equally in all places at all times. Instead, God manifests His presence in special ways. For example, God made His presence known in a special, powerful way in ancient Israel when He filled the Tabernacle, that focal point of worship. Exodus 40:34 tells us, *"Then the cloud covered the Tent of Meeting, and the glory of the Lord filled the tabernacle."* The early church experienced a similar manifestation of the powerful presence of God. Acts 4:31 says, *"After they prayed, the place where they were meeting was shaken. And they were all filled with the Holy Spirit and spoke the word of God boldly."* Christians today can also experience the presence of God in their lives. Paul instructs us to *"be filled with the Spirit"* in Ephesians 5:18. But in 2 Thessalonians 1:9, Paul also warns that those who fail to put their faith in Jesus Christ will be *"shut out from the presence of the Lord."* They will suffer eternal separation from God.

Invite Jesus to come into your heart today. He wants to be present in an unending relationship with you. The omnipresent God of the universe wants to be powerfully present in your life today and forever.

GOD IS HOLY

• • • • • • • •

Anyone who has traveled overseas knows the value of pure drinking water. Our missionary friends in Africa run their water through a highly sophisticated filter system in order to separate out the impurities. Once that water has been filtered, it's safe for consumption. It's been purified. In biblical terms, we might say that the water has been made "holy."

Holiness means that something or someone is separated from impurities—separated from sin. The Old Testament talks about holy objects or holy places, like the Temple, that were set apart from normal use for a distinct purpose.

The Bible also describes God as holy. Holiness is one aspect of His perfect character. However, in God's case there was nothing impure that had to be filtered out of His heart. He is inherently holy, completely set apart from evil. First John 1:5 says, *"God is light; in him there is no darkness at all."* Psalm 111:9 states, *"Holy and awesome is his name."* In those majestic words of Isaiah 6:3 the angels of heaven declare, *"Holy, holy, holy is the Lord Almighty; the whole earth is full of his glory."*

God is absolutely holy, completely pure in His character and untainted by sin. He has done no wrong. He can do no wrong. Therefore, He alone sets the standard of right and wrong. He is holy.

Unfortunately, because God is absolutely holy He cannot allow anything sinful to dwell in His presence.

Habakkuk 1:13 describes God by saying, *"Your eyes are too pure to look on evil; you cannot tolerate wrong."* This means that we, because of our sins whether great or small, are separated from God. Isaiah 59:2 warns, *"Your iniquities have separated you from your God; your sins have hidden his face from you, so that he will not hear."* We face an insurmountable dilemma.

Thankfully, God is able to remove the barrier of sin between us. In fact, He did so by sending Jesus to take our sins on Himself on the cross. Now, through faith in Jesus Christ alone, we can be completely purified. He makes us holy so that we can live with Him in heaven forever. Hebrews 10:10 says, *"We have been made holy through the sacrifice of the body of Jesus Christ once for all."*

Have you invited Jesus into your life to make you holy, acceptable to God for all eternity? Why not do that right now? Then, begin to grow to be more and more like Jesus Christ. Let your lifestyle match your new position in God's family. After all, God instructs us in 1 Peter 1:16, *"Be holy, because I am holy."*

GOD IS JUST

· · · · · · · ·

If you've ever served on jury duty you know how difficult it can be to determine guilt or innocence. The prosecuting attorney paints a convicting picture. You're convinced the accused is guilty. Then the defense attorney presents the evidence from a different angle, and you're equally confident that the accused is innocent. Sometimes justice isn't easy to determine in the courtroom. An unfair verdict is, of course, a tragedy. Don't you wish everything could be perfectly fair? Don't you wish that someone who knew all the facts could judge impartially and render true justice?

While life isn't always fair, there is a source of true justice. God is always fair. He is a just God. Justice is one of His defining attributes. Justice, or righteousness, refers to the concept that God is always consistent with His perfect standard of right and wrong. Psalm 89:14 says of God, *"Righteousness and justice are the foundation of your throne."* According to Revelation 15:3 the inhabitants of heaven call out, *"Great and marvelous are your deeds, Lord God Almighty. Just and true are your ways, King of the ages."*

Even though life may not seem fair, God will ultimately uphold justice. Jesus, in Luke 18:7-8, said, *"Will not God bring about justice for his chosen ones, who cry out to him day and night? I tell you, he will see that they get justice, and quickly."* God honors justice in this world, and even when things aren't fair here and now we know that in heaven God will eventually settle any injustices we experience in this world. Second Thessalonians 1:6-7 assures us, *"God is just: He will pay back trouble to those who trouble you and give relief to you who are troubled, and to us as well. This will happen when the Lord Jesus is revealed from heaven in blazing fire with his powerful angels."* As God's people, we look forward to that day in which God restores justice on earth.

However, God's justice can be a double-edged sword. We want God to treat us justly. But because He is just, He must judge our sins. We deserve to die forever because of our rebellious hearts and actions. But Jesus died in our place. Romans 3:25-26 tells us, *"God presented him as a sacrifice of atonement, through faith in his blood. He did this to demonstrate his justice . . . so as to be just and the one who justifies those who have faith in Jesus."*

Because God is just, He cannot simply overlook our sins. Instead, He transferred our sins to His Son. When we put our faith in Jesus, we are justly forgiven. First John 1:9 tells us, *"If we confess our sins, he is faithful and just and will forgive us our sins and purify us from all unrighteousness."* Why not put your faith in Jesus right now, thank Him for His justice, and receive His forgiveness?

GOD IS GOOD

· · · · · · · ·

God is good. It's so easy to say that phrase. It rolls off the tongue. God is good. But when it comes to life in the real world, we often wonder about the goodness of God. After all, there are plenty of not-so-good things in this world. Every time someone is diagnosed with cancer we wonder about God's goodness. If God is so good, why does He let bad things happen?

To answer this question we must recognize that God's goodness doesn't hinge on circumstances. His goodness is an aspect of His unchanging character. When we say that God is good, we mean that He is inherently kind and benevolent to all of His creatures. He desires our happiness and well being. But in order to provide for our happiness, He knew that it was necessary to create us in such a way that we could freely make choices. It's our sinful choices, not God's character, that account for the bad things that happen around us.

When sin entered the human race, disease, accidents, and hardships followed. These are the consequences of our rebellion against God. Granted, you may have experienced tragic events that were the results of someone else's sinful choices. There are victims—victims of drunk drivers, murder victims, victims of abuse. Still, these evils are the result of human sin, not a mark against God's goodness.

It might be that, for you, believing in the goodness of God is a real step of faith. Remember, the Bible clearly presents God as inherently good. For example, Psalm

119:68 says of God, *"You are good, and what you do is good."* God is good to His people, as Psalm 73:1 says: *"Surely God is good to Israel, to those who are pure in heart."* But God is also good even to those who reject Him. In Luke 6:35 Jesus said, *"Love your enemies, do good to them . . . and you will be sons of the Most High, because he is kind to the ungrateful and wicked."* Psalm 145:9 simply declares, *"The Lord is good to all; he has compassion on all he has made."*

Acknowledging the goodness of God is a step of faith, but it's a step that's supported with evidence. God has demonstrated His goodness to us in countless ways. Acts 14:17 says, *"He has shown kindness by giving you rain from heaven and crops in their seasons; he provides you with plenty of food and fills your hearts with joy."* James 1:17 reminds us, *"Every good and perfect gift is from above, coming down from the Father of the heavenly lights, who does not change like shifting shadows."* Anything good in life is a gift from God. We don't deserve His blessings, but because God is good He provides them for our pleasure.

The greatest proof of God's goodness is found in Jesus Christ. God sent Jesus, His Son, to die on the cross for our sins. Have you received Jesus into your heart? If so, thank Him for His goodness today.

GOD IS GRACIOUS

· · · · · · · ·

One of the great defining attributes of God is His grace. God blesses us even though we in no way deserve His blessings and could in no way earn them. Grace is God's unmerited favor.

We see God's grace at work in many ways. He's gracious not only to those who honor Him, but to all humankind. Titus 2:11 says, *"For the grace of God that brings salvation has appeared to all men."* We see God's grace in every good gift around us—the sunshine and rain, food and friendships, comforts, joys, and countless blessings every day. But not everyone responds to God's grace. In fact, Isaiah 26:10 tells us, *"Though grace is shown to the wicked, they do not learn righteousness; even in a land of uprightness they go on doing evil."* God's grace isn't based on our response but on His changeless character. He is constantly and consistently gracious.

Think about it for a moment. If it weren't for God's grace, none of us would be granted even a nanosecond to turn from our sins. Our sins deserve God's immediate wrath. But because God is a God of grace, He provides us with the opportunity to repent and be restored to full fellowship with Him.

God's grace also provides the means of forgiveness—the death of His own Son, Jesus Christ. Jesus paid the price for our sins, that is, He redeemed us. According to

Ephesians 1:7, *"In him we have redemption through his blood, the forgiveness of sins, in accordance with the riches of God's grace."* Because God is gracious to us, He redeemed us through Jesus' death on the cross. Our salvation is purely an act of God's grace. As Ephesians 2:8 tells us, *"It is by grace you have been saved through faith."* Romans 3:23-24 puts it this way: *"For all have sinned and fall short of the glory of God, and are justified freely by his grace through the redemption that came by Christ Jesus."* Because God is a God of grace, we can be saved forever from our sins and their consequences.

But God's grace doesn't end with our salvation. John 1:16 says, *"From the fullness of his grace we have all received one blessing after another."* We are the blessed recipients of God's endless grace.

Because God is a God of grace, we can receive His gracious gift of salvation through faith in Jesus Christ. Have you received God's Son into your heart? Why not accept the grace He offers you today? Then, when you've received God's grace, learn to be gracious to those around you. Let grace characterize your hearts, actions, and words. As Colossians 4:6 reminds us, *"Let your conversation be always full of grace."* God is gracious. Let's follow His example in the way we treat others.

GOD IS FAITHFUL

....

I've never been to Yellowstone National Park, but someday I'd sure like to see that beautiful slice of God's creation. One attraction to Yellowstone would certainly be Old Faithful. This amazing geyser spouts steaming hot water over a hundred feet in the air about every ninety minutes. It received its name because of the consistency of its eruptions.

Isn't it comforting to know that God is faithful? He consistently and constantly cares for us. We can depend on Him to fulfill His purposes in this world and in our lives. In the middle of a book that describes human sadness, Lamentations 3:22-23 reminds us, *"Because of the Lord's great love we are not consumed, for his compassions never fail. They are new every morning; great is your faithfulness."*

Faithfulness is an attribute of God's perfect character. In fact, the Bible often links God's faithfulness with some of His other attributes. For example, Psalm 36:5 says, *"Your love, O Lord, reaches to the heavens, your faithfulness to the skies."* Hosea 11:12 refers to God as the *"faithful Holy One."* Hebrews 2:17 describes Jesus as our *"merciful and faithful high priest."* First John 1:9 tells us that God is *"faithful and just and will forgive us our sins."* Revelation 19:11 attributes the name *"Faithful and True"* to Jesus Christ. God's faithfulness is intertwined with His love, holiness, mercy, justice, truth, and every other aspect of His divine character. He is inherently faithful.

Three-Minute Theology

To say that God is faithful means that He always keeps His promises. According to Hebrews 11:11, Abraham *"considered him faithful who had made the promise"* and God did keep His promise by blessing Abraham and his descendants. Hebrews 10:23 assures us, *"He who promised is faithful."* God has given us countless promises in His Word, and because He is faithful we can be confident that He will keep every promise.

What are some of your favorite Bible promises? I like Joshua 1:9, where God promised, *"The Lord your God will be with you wherever you go,"* and Hebrews 13:5, where God said, *"Never will I leave you; never will I forsake you."* I know that God is constantly present in my life because He promised to always be at my side and He is faithful to His promises. Another wonderful promise that God made to us is to hear us when we pray and to save us when we trust in His Son, Jesus Christ. Romans 10:13 promises, *"Everyone who calls on the name of the Lord will be saved."* Have you called out to God for His saving work in your life? If so, He has already kept His promise and saved you from eternal death. You now have eternal life in Christ because God is faithful.

GOD IS LOVE

· · · · · · · ·

One of most cherished attributes of God is His love. God is love. But what does this mean? The Bible describes love as an unconditional commitment and unending compassion. We're to love our spouse unconditionally. We're to keep on loving one another in spite of our faults. We're to love God with our whole heart, mind, and strength.

God displayed His love long before He created us. Love existed within the triune godhead from eternity past. In Matthew 3:17, God the Father declared, *"This is my Son, whom I love; with him I am well pleased."* Jesus, in John 14:31, said, *"The world must learn that I love the Father and that I do exactly what my Father has commanded me."* This mutual love within the trinity shows us that love is an inherent attribute of God.

While it's understandable that there would be love between God the Father and God the Son, it's absolutely amazing that God would love us. When Jesus prayed to God the Father, He described the Father's love for us. John 17:23 says, *"May they be brought to complete unity to let the world know that you sent me and have loved them even as you have loved me."* God the Father loves us just like He loves His own Son! He loves us in spite of our sin. John 3:16 says, *"For God so loved the world that he gave his one and only Son, that whoever believes in him shall not perish but have eternal life."* God loves us so much that He sent His beloved Son, Jesus, to die in our place.

Three-Minute Theology

Likewise, Jesus Christ Himself loves us. He willingly gave His life for us. First John 3:16 tells us, *"This is how we know what love is: Jesus Christ laid down his life for us."* Have you invited Jesus into your heart? Thank Him for His love, His sacrificial death, and His eternal forgiveness. He loves you so much that He wants to spend forever with you.

Because God has shown His unconditional commitment and compassion for us, we should respond by loving God in return. In Mark 12:30 Jesus said, *"Love the Lord your God with all your soul and with all your mind and with all your strength."* And if we truly love God, we'll love others as well. Jesus, in Mark 12:31, went on to say, *"Love your neighbor as yourself."* Because God loves us, we should love Him and we should love others. While this is easy to say, it's not always easy to do. Will you spend time with God, enjoying His presence and honoring His Word? Will you treat others with respect, care, and compassion no matter how they respond? Will you and I be loving disciples of Jesus Christ? Remember, in John 13:35 Jesus said, *"By this all men will know that you are my disciples, if you love one another."* Ask Jesus to be your Savior, and then ask Him to make you a lover.

JESUS CHRIST OUR LORD

JESUS' DEITY

∙ ∙ ∙ ∙ ∙ ∙ ∙ ∙

Jesus is God. This statement is the necessary beginning point in our understanding of the identity and power of Jesus Christ. Jesus is God.

People around us describe Jesus in many ways. Some say that He was a great teacher, a great care-giver, a great man, or even a great revolutionary. Recently I saw a book that described Jesus as a great therapist! While Jesus was a great teacher, care-giver, man, revolutionary, and even the greatest therapist, if we stop with these descriptions we fail to understand who Jesus really is. Jesus was great in many ways, but greatest of all is the fact that Jesus is God.

In John 10:30, Jesus told His critics, *"I and the Father are one."* He was claiming to be uniquely related to God the Father, equal to God in every way. We know that this was what Jesus was saying, because His critics attempted to stone Him to death for claiming to be God. This wasn't the only time that Jesus claimed to be equal with God the Father. He said that to honor Him is to honor the Father (John 5:23), to believe in Him is to believe in the Father (John 12:45), to know Him is to know the Father (John 14:7), to hate Him is to hate the Father (John 15:23), and to receive Him is to receive the Father (Mark 9:37). Clearly, Jesus believed that He was God and made this claim over and over again.

It's one thing to claim that you're God. It's quite another to actually be God. Jesus claimed to be God, but

He backed His claims with His miraculous power. He healed the sick, walked on water, fed the multitudes, and even raised the dead. God the Father would never give such amazing power to someone who falsely claimed to be God. Jesus claimed Himself to be divine, and His miraculous power verified His claim.

Furthermore, because Jesus is God, He rightly accepted expressions of worship. For example, the disciple Thomas fell on his knees before the resurrected Jesus and, according to John 20:28, declared, *"My Lord and my God."* Jesus affirmed this declaration of worship, and His resurrection powerfully proved His deity.

In Colossians 1:15-16, the apostle Paul described Jesus as *"the image of the invisible God, the firstborn over all creation,"* and states that Jesus made all created things. Therefore, Jesus Himself could not have been created. He is eternal. He is God.

Because Jesus is God, He is well capable of tackling our greatest needs. Of course, our greatest need is for salvation, the eternal forgiveness of our sins. Jesus met that need by dying on the cross. You can turn to Jesus today for salvation, and you can trust Him with your life. After all, Jesus Christ is God.

JESUS' INCARNATION

One of the greatest truths of the Bible and one of the greatest mysteries of the Christian faith is the fact that God became a man. The second member of the triune Godhead, Jesus, took on for all time and eternity a sinless human nature. This act of God becoming a man is called the incarnation, a word that means "in the flesh." God came to live among us in the flesh.

Most often our minds turn to Bethlehem's manger when we think about the incarnation. But the incarnation began in eternity past in the counsel of Almighty God. Nine months before His birth, Jesus was conceived in the womb of Mary. The conception of Jesus' human body and the union of the human and divine natures was truly a miracle.

The apostle John referred to Jesus as the "Word," a term that implies the wisdom and oneness of Jesus within the triune Godhead. John 1:1 says that *"the Word was God."* Jesus is God. But then in John 1:14 the apostle states, *"The Word became flesh and made his dwelling among us. We have seen his glory, the glory of the One and Only, full of grace and truth."* The Word was God, and the Word became flesh. God and man were forever joined in the person of Jesus Christ.

The incarnation is a great mystery. How could the infinite become finite? How could the Creator become a part of His creation? How could our all-powerful God grow weary, thirsty, and hungry? How could the eternal God die on a cross? We'll probably never understand the incarnation fully. Even the writers of the New Testament had to search for words to describe this unique work of God. Paul, in Philippians 2:6-7, said that Jesus Christ existed *"in very nature"* as God, but *"made himself nothing, taking the very nature of a servant and being made in human likeness."* In Colossians 2:9 he wrote, *"For in Christ all the fullness of the Deity lives in bodily form."*

In his fascination with the incarnation, the apostle John in 1 John 1:1 described Jesus as *"That which was from the beginning, which we have heard, which we have seen with our eyes, which we have looked at and our hands have touched."* The incarnation is truly a mystery, but one with practical value.

We might ask, "Why would the God of heavenly splendor humbly enter into our human existence?" The answer lies in His love for us. Because of our sins, we are separated eternally from God. But because of His love, He came into our world, He became a man, and He died in our place. Only a human being could die for human sins. Only an eternal being could die for a whole world's sins. Jesus is the eternal Son of God who became a man so that He could die for our sins. Since Jesus did this for you, why wouldn't you invite Him into your life to be your Savior and your Lord?

JESUS' IMPECCABILITY

· · · · · · · ·

Nobody's perfect! Sometimes those two words are the only excuse we can offer when we let someone down. We say it at work. We say it to our spouses. We might even be tempted to say it to a judge when we get a traffic ticket. After all, nobody's perfect. Well, not exactly. There is one man who is perfectly perfect. That man is the God-man, Jesus Christ.

The sinlessness of Jesus is an essential doctrine of the Christian faith. After all, we couldn't rely on another sinner to take our sins away. Only a sinless Savior could pay the penalty for our sins.

The New Testament is adamant about the sinless perfection of Jesus Christ. In spite of intense temptation, Jesus never sinned. Satan did his best to lure Jesus into sin. For forty days Jesus endured Satan's attacks in the wilderness, culminating in three powerful temptations. Satan tempted Jesus to depend on His own power instead of the Father's provision by making bread out of stones. Satan tempted Jesus to test the Father's protecting power by casting Himself off a high point of the Temple. Satan also tempted Jesus to forsake the Father's plan by receiving all the kingdoms of the world without going to the cross. But in each and every temptation, Jesus responded in obedience to the Word of God, even quoting it in the face of Satan's onslaught. Matthew 4:10 tells us that, at the end of this intense period of temptation, Jesus dismissed the devil, saying, *"Away from me, Satan!"* Jesus was tempted more intensely than any man in history, yet He never succumbed. He is sinless. He's perfect.

When Jesus' opponents sought to find fault in Him they were sorely disappointed. Jesus even asked them, in John 8:46, *"Can any of you prove me guilty of sin?"* His critics could find nothing wrong in Jesus. They even had to trump up false charges at Jesus' trial in order to send Him to the cross.

Hebrews 4:15 states that Jesus was *"tempted in every way, just as we are—yet was without sin."* Jesus never sinned. While we know that Jesus didn't sin, it also makes sense to conclude that Jesus couldn't sin. After all, Jesus is God in the flesh, and God cannot sin. The idea that Jesus couldn't have sinned is called the "impeccability" of Christ. Theologians debate this point, but there is no debate about Jesus' holy character and sinless life.

Aren't you glad that Jesus never sinned? In 2 Corinthians 5:21 Paul wrote, *"God made him who had no sin to be sin for us, so that in him we might become the righteousness of God."* Because Jesus was sinless, He could take our sins on Himself on the cross. Would you like to have your sins completely forgiven? Turn to Jesus Christ by faith. He alone is our sinless Savior.

JESUS' CRUCIFIXION

It was certainly a dark day in the history of humankind. Jesus, God in the flesh, hung nailed to a wooden cross.

How did this come about? After all, Jesus proclaimed a message of God's love. He healed sick people. He delivered those who were controlled by demons. He fed the multitudes. He taught truth and offered hope. Why would anyone want to kill a man like this?

To be sure, Jesus didn't die because of His own sins. He was sinless. Instead, Jesus died in our place. He died to take our sins away. While we might want to blame Jesus' enemies or the Roman soldiers who actually carried out the act of crucifixion, we know that ultimately we are each responsible for Jesus' death. Our sins, coupled with His love for us, compelled Jesus to die on the cross.

John 10:17-18 reveals an interesting perspective on Jesus' crucifixion. Jesus said, *"The reason my Father loves me is that I lay down my life—only to take it up again. No one takes it from me, but I lay it down of my own accord."* While the crucifixion was a tragic day in history, it was also the fulfillment of a plan that began way back in eternity.

So, what did Jesus' crucifixion accomplish? Jesus' death paved the way for us to establish a personal relationship with God. First Peter 3:18 tells us, *"Christ died for sins, once for all, the righteous for the unrighteous, to bring you to God."* Our sins have separated us from God. While we'd like to think that God could simply overlook our sins, God's attribute of justice demands a payment, a punishment for sin. He can't simply wink at our sins and walk away. However, God loves us too much to leave us stranded in our sins. That's why He sent His Son, Jesus. Jesus died for our sins to bring us back into fellowship with God.

The crucifixion doesn't make sense to the unbelieving mind. In 1 Corinthians 1:23-24, Paul described the cross of Jesus Christ as a *"stumbling block"* and *"foolishness"* to unbelievers, but to those who believe in Jesus the cross is *"the power of God."*

Is it any wonder, then, that the Bible describes our faith relationship with Jesus Christ as crucifixion? Galatians 2:20 says, *"I have been crucified with Christ and I no longer live, but Christ lives in me. The life I live in the body, I live by faith in the Son of God, who loved me and gave himself for me."* Jesus died on a cross to pay for my sins. When I receive Jesus as my Savior, I accept His crucifixion. In essence, I'm saying that my old life of sin was nailed to Jesus' cross. Now I can live a new life of faith and obedience to Jesus. Is the cross foolishness to you, or have you staked your life to the crucifixion of Jesus Christ? Why not turn to Him today?

JESUS' RESURRECTION

· · · · · · · ·

Did you know that the apostle Paul gave away the secret to destroying the Christian faith? In 1 Corinthians 15:14 he wrote, *"If Christ has not been raised, our preaching is useless and so is your faith."* The resurrection of Jesus Christ is the lynchpin of the Christian faith. Without the resurrection, Christianity crumbles like a house of cards.

So why would Paul give away this secret? Won't skeptics attack Christianity at this most critical point? The fact is, skeptics have indeed attempted to discredit Christianity by denying the resurrection of Jesus Christ. But the evidence for Jesus' resurrection is so compelling that it's withstood centuries of attack. No one has been able to disprove the resurrection. Furthermore, many who have attempted to do so have ended up turning to Jesus Christ, convinced that He's alive. As Christians, we need never fear the most intense scrutiny of our faith. Jesus is alive, and because He rose from the dead the Christian faith is more than secure. It's advancing around the world.

Now, we must be careful to understand what the Bible means when it says that Jesus is alive. We've all lost loved ones through death. Sometimes at a funeral I'll hear someone say that their loved one will always be alive in their memories and in their hearts. This is a real and comforting sentiment. But when we say that

Jesus is alive, we mean much more than that He's alive in our sentiments. He is actually alive physically. He rose physically from the grave. When Jesus' followers went to His tomb three days after the crucifixion, the grave was empty.

Furthermore, Jesus met physically with His followers after the resurrection. He spoke with them, ate with them, taught them, and comforted them. These appearances of Jesus took place on several occasions over several weeks before Jesus ascended into heaven. As a result, these men and women were transformed. Cowards became courageous preachers of the truth. Doubters became martyrs because Jesus is alive.

So what does the resurrection of Jesus Christ mean to us today? Romans 4:25 says, *"He was delivered over to death for our sins and was raised to life for our justification."* Our eternal salvation depends on Jesus' resurrection. If you've received Jesus by faith, your sins are forgiven and you have resurrection life. In fact, through faith in Jesus you have resurrection power available to help you live for God today. Ephesians 1:18-20 encourages us to know God's *"incomparably great power"* that's at work in our lives and to recognize that this power for living is identical to *"the working of his mighty strength, which he exerted in Christ when he raised him from the dead."* Jesus' resurrection is the basis of our faith and the basis of our victory over sin day by day. Have you received the risen Christ into your life?

JESUS' RETURN

....

To a small child, a father's words can be very comforting. As Dad is heading out the door for another business trip, he says, "Don't worry, I'll be back soon." The son or daughter looks forward to Dad's return, and the possibility of a small gift that Dad may have purchased along the way.

We're like children in many ways. Jesus said that we have to become like little children in order to enter into His kingdom. Childlike faith is essential. Jesus also offered words of comfort for His children when He went back to heaven. In essence, He said, "Don't worry, I'll be back soon." More specifically, in John 14:2-3 He told His disciples, *"In my Father's house are many mansions; if it were not so, I would have told you. I am going there to prepare a place for you. And if I go and prepare a place for you, I will come back and take you to be with me that you also may be where I am."* Jesus is coming back!

The return of Jesus Christ could take place at any moment. We say that His return is "imminent." Titus 2:13 instructs us to live godly lives *"while we wait for the blessed hope—the glorious appearing of our great God and Savior, Jesus Christ."* Jesus Christ will appear at a time unknown to us but known in heaven, and when He comes He will come quickly. For example, in Revelation 22:12 Jesus said, *"Behold, I am coming soon. My reward is with me, and I will give to everyone according to what he has done."* Jesus is coming at any time, and like a father who brings his child a gift after a long business trip, He even promised to bring us rewards. Jesus is coming again. He could come today.

Because Jesus could come at any moment, we want to be ready at every moment. This means that we should live our lives with vigilance. In Matthew 24:42 Jesus said, *"Therefore keep watch, because you do not know on what day your Lord will appear."* Keeping watch means to keep looking up in anticipation of Jesus' return. It also means to keep looking inward to make sure that our lives are consistently conformed to God's will. You may want to ask yourself, "Where will Jesus find me when He returns? What will Jesus find me doing when He comes back?" First John 3:2-3 tells us, *"We know that when he appears, we shall be like him, for we shall see him as he is. Everyone who has this hope in him purifies himself, just as he is pure."* Since we look forward to Jesus' return, we'll want to live pure lives day in and day out. We want Jesus to find us living in obedient devotion when He comes to take us home to heaven.

Are you looking forward to Jesus' return? Are you ready? The best step you can take to prepare for Jesus' second coming is to ask Jesus into your heart today. He died to take away your sins and give you eternal life. Why not accept Him today? Then, begin to live a life of practical purity as you look forward to Jesus' return.

THE HOLY SPIRIT

THE INDWELLING WORK OF THE HOLY SPIRIT

· · · · · · · ·

Outward appearances can be deceiving. It's what's inside that counts. When we look at some of the plain, ordinary people around us we may fail to perceive the presence of Almighty God. But God the Holy Spirit lives inside every true Christian. We call this special presence the indwelling work of the Holy Spirit.

The Spirit's indwelling is a personal connection, an intimate relationship that He establishes with those who've placed their faith in Jesus Christ. In Romans 8:9 the apostle Paul wrote, *"You, however, are controlled not by the sinful nature but by the Spirit, if the Spirit of God lives in you. And if anyone does not have the Spirit of Christ, he does not belong to Christ."* In other words, the Holy Spirit lives in every true believer. He has a personal, indwelling relationship with us.

God's people haven't always enjoyed the privilege of the Holy Spirit's indwelling work. In John 14:17 Jesus told His disciples about their relationship with the Holy Spirit, saying, *"You know him, for he lives with you and will be in you."* Prior to Jesus' death the Holy Spirit lived with God's people. After Jesus returned to heaven the Holy Spirit came to actually live inside God's people in a permanent, intimate relationship. Jesus, in John 14:16-17, also told His disciples, *"I will ask the Father, and he will give you another Counselor to be with you forever—the Spirit of truth."* At the moment of salvation the Holy Spirit enters our lives in a permanent union. He lives in us right here, right now, and forever!

Because the Holy Spirit of God lives inside us as Christians, we have access to His divine power. For example, the Holy Spirit enables us to understand spiritual truth. First Corinthians 2:12 tells us, *"We have not received the spirit of the world but the Spirit who is from God, that we may understand what God has freely given us."* The Holy Spirit living in us helps us know truth from error, right from wrong. He also assures us of our right standing in God's sight. Second Corinthians 5:5 says, *"Now it is God who has made us for this very purpose and has given us the Spirit as a deposit, guaranteeing what is to come."*

Since the Holy Spirit lives inside us, we'll want to live pure and holy lives. First Corinthians 6:19-20 states, *"Do you not know that your body is a temple of the Holy Spirit, who is in you, whom you have received from God? You are not your own; you were bought at a price. Therefore honor God with your body."* Because the Holy Spirit lives inside us, God is present no matter what we do or think. Shouldn't God's personal presence motivate us to live pure lives for Him?

Only the blood of Jesus Christ can purify us from sin. Receive Jesus as your Savior today. Accept His forgiveness and you too will benefit from the presence of the indwelling Holy Spirit of God.

THE BAPTIZING WORK OF THE HOLY SPIRIT

• • • • • • • •

When Jesus was about to begin His public ministry, John the Baptist burst on the scene calling people to repentance. His mission was to point people to the long anticipated Messiah. In Matthew 3:11 John the Baptist said, *"I baptize you with water for repentance. But after me will come one who is more powerful than I, whose sandals I am not fit to carry. He will baptize you with the Holy Spirit and with fire."* Spirit baptism is a precious truth in the life of God's people.

The baptizing work of the Holy Spirit didn't take place during Jesus' earthly ministry. In fact, after His crucifixion and resurrection Jesus still spoke about Spirit baptism as a future event. In Acts 1:5 Jesus told His disciples, *"John baptized with water, but in a few days you will be baptized with the Holy Spirit."* That baptizing work of the Holy Spirit took place on the Day of Pentecost as described in the second chapter of Acts. At that moment the Holy Spirit took up permanent residence in the lives of each of Jesus' followers and empowered them for service. Later in the book of Acts a similar event took place. When Gentiles first received the gospel, they too were baptized by the Holy Spirit. The apostle Peter described this event in Acts 11:15-16, saying, *"As I began to speak, the Holy Spirit came on them as he had come on us at the beginning. Then I remembered what the Lord had said: 'John baptized with water, but you will be baptized with the Holy Spirit.'"*

Ever since these initial experiences of Spirit baptism, every believer has been baptized by the Holy Spirit of God. An important verse that helps us understand the nature of Spirit baptism is found in 1 Corinthians 12:13, which says, *"For we were all baptized by one Spirit into one body—whether Jews or Greeks, slave or free—and we were all given the one Spirit to drink."* According to this verse, all of us who are believers in Jesus Christ have been baptized by the Holy Spirit. Therefore, Spirit baptism must take place at the moment we receive Jesus as our Savior. We need look for no second encounter with Spirit baptism, but can accept by faith that we have already been baptized by the Spirit. This baptizing work of the Holy Spirit includes His personal and powerful work inside us. It also includes the Spirit's work of uniting us to Jesus Christ and His church. Through Spirit baptism we have been placed into the body of Christ. This means that we are spiritually connected with every other believer. We have something—some One—in common. We have a common Lord, a common mission, a common love. We have fellowship with one another and with our Lord Jesus Christ.

Have you received Jesus as your Savior? If so, you can be encouraged to know that the Holy Spirit is working inside you. Through Spirit baptism you've been forever connected to Jesus Christ and His body, the church.

THE FILLING WORK OF THE HOLY SPIRIT

• • • • • • • •

Most people would say that they want to be in charge of their own lives, to be in control, to sit in the driver's seat. But the fact is that self-control often spills over into a total loss of control. For example, anger may control some people. We might say that such an individual is full of rage, meaning that anger controls his or her life. On the positive side, we all know some people that are full of love. Love seems to be the controlling factor in their words and actions. That which fills us controls us.

Ephesians 5:18 tells us, *"Do not get drunk on wine, which leads to debauchery. Instead, be filled with the Spirit."* As followers of Jesus Christ, we're to be filled—or controlled—by the Holy Spirit. At the moment we put our faith in Jesus Christ, the Holy Spirit of God came to live within us. He established a permanent, indwelling relationship. His indwelling presence never changes. However, even though the Holy Spirit lives in us, He isn't always in control of our lives. We must cooperate with the Spirit when it comes to His filling work. Our goal is to be constantly controlled by the Spirit.

So how can we cooperate with the Holy Spirit inside us so that He's in control? First of all, Ephesians 4:30 warns us, *"Do not grieve the Holy Spirit of God."* We certainly grieve the Spirit when we engage willfully in sin. Sinful habits will prevent us from experiencing the filling of the Holy Spirit. Then we read in 1 Thessalonians 5:19, *"Do not put out the Spirit's fire."* We douse the Spirit's work in our lives when we resist His leading. When we determine to be in charge of our own decisions we fail to follow the Spirit's gentle guidance. Finally, Galatians 5:16 says, *"Walk in the Spirit, and you will not gratify the desires of the flesh."* These verses point us toward the basic concepts of obeying and yielding. If we remain obedient to God's commands, not engaging in sinful practices, and if we yield ourselves to the Spirit's leading, the Holy Spirit will fill us, bless us, and use us.

So, then, what would a Spirit filled life look like? The book of Acts frequently refers to believers who were filled with the Holy Spirit. For example, Acts 4:31 says, *"After they prayed, the place where they were meeting was shaken. And they were all filled with the Holy Spirit and spoke the word of God boldly."* Acts 11:24 describes Barnabas as *"a good man, full of the Holy Spirit and faith,"* through whom *"a great number of people were brought to the Lord."* When we're filled with the Spirit of God we'll be bold in sharing our faith with others. Ephesians 5:18-21 tells us that when we're filled with the Spirit we'll also *"sing and make music"* in our hearts and we'll *"submit to one another out of reverence for Christ."* Sharing, singing, submitting—these and other characteristics reveal the fullness of the Holy Spirit in our lives. Why not turn your life over to God today? Yield to Him and allow His Holy Spirit to take control of your life.

THE EMPOWERING WORK OF THE HOLY SPIRIT

· · · · · · · ·

Whenever there's a power outage we instantly become aware of how much we depend on electricity. No lights, no heat, no refrigeration, no television—a lack of power can cripple whole communities. Even more important than electrical power is spiritual power. Without the power of God at work in our lives we'd come apart at the seams in no time. Aren't you glad that Jesus Christ promised to provide us with power for living the Christian life?

In Acts 1:8 Jesus told His followers, *"You will receive power when the Holy Spirit comes on you; and you will be my witnesses in Jerusalem, and in all Judea and Samaria, and to the ends of the earth."* God gives spiritual power to His people, and He does so through the indwelling Holy Spirit.

The Holy Spirit's power should be evident in the way we share our faith. In 1 Corinthians 2:4-5 the apostle Paul said, *"My message and my preaching were not with wise and persuasive words, but with a demonstration of the Spirit's power, so that your faith might not rest on men's wisdom, but on God's power."* We dare not rely on clever gospel presentations to convince people of God's truth. Instead, we should rely on the Holy Spirit to take even our weakest words and use them powerfully in people's hearts.

Another way in which the Holy Spirit's power can be evident in our lives is through a personal sense of peace and hope that we receive from God. Romans 15:13 says, *"May the God of hope fill you with all joy and peace as you trust in him, so that you may overflow with hope by the power of the Holy Spirit."* The power of the Holy Spirit gives us inner peace even when the rest of life is in turmoil.

Still another way in which the Holy Spirit displays His power in our lives is through spiritual gifts. According to 1 Corinthians 12:7, every Christian has received at least one spiritual gift, an ability to serve others supernaturally. This verse says, *"Now to each one the manifestation of the Spirit is given for the common good."* These spiritual gifts are distributed by the Holy Spirit to produce unity and maturity within the body of Christ. Ephesians 4:12-13 says that the Holy Spirit has given spiritual gifts *"to prepare God's people for works of service, so that the body of Christ may be built up until we all reach unity in the faith and in the knowledge of the Son of God and become mature, attaining to the whole measure of the fullness of Christ."* Whether we have the spiritual gift of teaching, serving, encouraging, giving, leading or any of the other gifts described in the New Testament, we have been given divine power to glorify God and build up Christ's church.

How are you using your spiritual gifts? How are you seeing the power of the Holy Spirit flow through you? By the power of the Holy Spirit who lives in us we can all share our faith effectively, experience inner peace, and contribute to the health of the church.

THE SPIRIT WORLD

THE NATURE OF ANGELS

• • • • • • • •

When you think of angels what image comes to your mind? Chubby little babies with wings? White-robed beings from another dimension? Imaginary beings from the pages of mythology? The Bible is our only reliable source for understanding the nature of angels.

The Bible, in fact, describes angels as real, supernatural beings that were created by God. Psalm 148, verses 2 and 5 say, *"Praise him, all his angels, praise him, all his heavenly host . . . . Let them praise the name of the Lord, for he commanded and they were created."* Colossians 1:16 attributes the creation of angelic beings specifically to God the Son, saying, *"For by him all things were created: things in heaven and on earth, visible and invisible, whether thrones or powers or rulers or authorities; all things were created by him and for him."* Angels, therefore, are real spirit beings that are distinct from human beings. People don't become angels when they die. Angels are a unique part of God's creation.

Angels are spirit beings. They don't possess physical bodies. Hebrews 1:14 says, *"Are not all angels ministering spirits sent to serve those who will inherit salvation?"* In Ephesians 6:12 Paul, speaking of fallen angels, says, *"For our struggle is not against flesh and blood, but against the rulers, against the authorities, against the powers of this dark world and against the spiritual forces of evil in the heavenly realms."*

Although angels don't possess physical bodies, they can appear in physical form. The prophet Isaiah saw certain angels called Seraphim surrounding the throne of God. In Isaiah 6:2 he wrote, *"Above him were seraphs, each with six wings: With two wings they covered their faces, with two they covered their feet, and with two they were flying."* Another prophet, Ezekiel, saw a different class of angels called Cherubim. Ezekiel 1:5-6 says, *"In appearance their form was that of a man, but each of them had four faces and four wings."* In the New Testament angels appeared at the time of Jesus' birth and at the empty tomb after His resurrection. Matthew 28:3 describes one of these angels, saying, *"His appearance was like lightning, and his clothes were white as snow."* When angels appear in physical form, their appearance seems to vary depending on the circumstances.

As impressive as an angelic appearance would be, the Bible warns us not to worship angels. Angels are created beings. Only God, the Creator, deserves worship. We should never worship angels, but we can learn from angels how to worship God. Like the angelic beings in Revelation 5:12 we should cry out, *"Worthy is the Lamb, who was slain."* Why not open your heart to worship the Lamb of God, Jesus Christ today.

THE MINISTRY OF ANGELS

• • • • • • • •

An unhappy husband once said, "My wife's a real angel—she's always harping about something!" Obviously this husband needs a course in building a happy marriage. He also needs a course about angels. If we think that angels are simply sitting around heaven playing harps, we've clearly not read the Bible. The Bible, our only really reliable source about angels, paints a completely different picture. Angels are specially created spirit beings who play a significant role in God's plan. In basic terms, angels are both messengers and ministers.

First, we discover from the Bible that angels are messengers. In fact, the term "angel" comes from the Greek word for messenger. One specific messenger angel named Gabriel appears in both the Old and New Testaments. In Daniel 9:22 Gabriel said to the prophet, *"Daniel, I have now come to give you insight and understanding."* God used Gabriel to deliver His special revelation to Daniel. This same angelic messenger delivered the news of the coming birth of John the Baptist, telling his father Zechariah *"I am Gabriel. I stand in the presence of God, and I have been sent to speak to you and to tell you this good news"* (Luke 1:19). Soon afterward, Gabriel spoke to Mary and announced the coming of Jesus. In Luke 1:35 Gabriel said to Mary, *"The Holy Spirit will come upon you, and the power of the Most High will overshadow you. So the holy one to be born will be called the Son of God."* An unnamed angel announced the birth of Jesus to shepherds in the field around Bethlehem. Luke 2:10-11 quotes this angel's message, *"Do not be afraid. I bring you good news of great joy that will be for all the people. Today in the town of David a Savior has been born to you; he is Christ the Lord."* After Jesus' resurrection an angel announced to the women at the empty tomb, *"Do not be afraid, for I know that you are looking for Jesus, who was crucified. He is not here; he has risen, just as he said"* (Matthew 28:5-6). Angels have indeed been entrusted with some of the most amazing messages from heaven.

Second, the Bible tells us that angels are ministers. They serve God and God's people. Hebrews 1:14 says, *"Are not all angels ministering spirits sent to serve those who will inherit salvation?"* God employs angels to offer praise, to mete out punishment, and to protect His people. In Luke 22:43 we read that while Jesus poured out His soul in the Garden of Gethsemane, *"An angel from heaven appeared to him and strengthened him."* Psalm 91:11 assures us, *"He will command his angels concerning you to guard you in all your ways."* Angels minister to both God and God's people.

It's comforting to know that God cares for us in so many ways. We can trust Him with our whole hearts. Have you trusted Jesus Christ? Why not put your faith in Him today!

SATAN

· · · · · · · ·

Sometimes we hear people excuse their bad behavior by saying, "The devil made me do it." While there's no justification for blaming Satan for our personal sins, Satan is a real being who does entice us to reject God's holy standard for our lives.

But where did Satan come from? Satan is a created spirit being, and since everything in God's original creation was "good," Satan at one time was one of the holy angels. Ezekiel 28:12-13 says of Satan, *"You were the model of perfection, full of wisdom and perfect in beauty. You were in Eden, the garden of God."* Verse 15 goes on to say, *"You were blameless in your ways from the day you were created till wickedness was found in you."* Known as "Lucifer," or the "Morning Star," Satan became proud of his beauty, his position, and his power. Isaiah 14:12-14 describes his fall, saying, *"How you have fallen from heaven, O morning star, son of the dawn! . . . You said in your heart, 'I will ascend to heaven; I will raise my throne above the stars of God; . . . I will ascend above the tops of the clouds; I will make myself like the Most High.'"*

When Satan fell, he enticed other angelic beings to follow him in his rebellion against God. He also attacked the first man and woman, Adam and Eve, by tempting Eve to disobey God's command in the Garden of Eden. Ever since his fall, Satan has been the archenemy of God and God's people.

Jesus described Satan as the "enemy" in Matthew 13:39, and in John 8:44 Jesus calls Satan "the devil," a "murderer," and a "liar." Satan wants to deceive us into thinking that we don't need God, thereby tripping us up and destroying our lives. Satan attacks God's people by deceiving us, distorting the truth, and distracting us from pure devotion to God. Satan is a cunning enemy who often makes his temptations appear to be good and beneficial. Second Corinthians 11:14 says that *"Satan himself masquerades as an angel of light."* We need to be constantly on guard against the devil. First Peter 5:8-9 warns, *"Be self-controlled and alert. Your enemy the devil prowls around like a roaring lion looking for someone to devour."*

While Satan is a formidable enemy, he's also a defeated foe. First John 3:8 states, *"The reason the Son of God appeared was to destroy the devil's work."* Jesus defeated Satan by dying on the cross and rising from the dead. When we put our faith in Jesus Christ we enter into Jesus' victory over Satan. James 4:7 tells us, *"Submit yourselves, then, to God. Resist the devil, and he will flee from you."* When Satan tempts us to sin, we can resist him in the name of our Savior, Jesus Christ, and gain victory over temptation. However, we can't expect to have victory by our own power. We need Jesus. Why not invite Jesus into your heart and ask Him to give you victory today?

SATAN'S DEFEAT

• • • • • • • •

Everyone wants to be on a winning team. As sports fans, we cheer for our team to win the Pennant or make it to the Super Bowl. In business, we want our work teams to succeed and excel in the marketplace. In the bigger issues of life and eternity it's reassuring to Christians to know that we're on the winning side. We're part of an age-long spiritual conflict. Satan is waging war against God. Sin stands in opposition to holiness. The spiritual battlefield includes our hearts. But when we give our hearts to Jesus, we share in His victory over evil.

Jesus' victory means that Satan is a defeated foe. The Bible tells us that Satan was once one of the holy angels, but he became proud and rebelled against God. His fall ushered sin into the universe, and each of us has participated in sinning against God. We'd be hopelessly and eternally lost except for the saving grace of God.

First John 3:8 tells us, *"The reason the Son of God appeared was to destroy the devil's work."* By His grace, God the Father sent His Son, Jesus Christ, into this world to undo the evil that Satan has inflicted. This was God's plan all along. Immediately after Adam and Eve followed Satan's temptation and disobeyed God, God declared His plan to counteract Satan's destructive acts. God told the serpent that the seed of the woman, a descendant of Eve, would destroy him. In Genesis 3:15 God said, *"I will put enmity between you and the woman, and between your offspring and hers; he will crush your head, and you will strike his heel."* At the cross it appeared that Satan had won a great victory by striking the heel of the Son of God. But in that sacrificial death Jesus instead crushed Satan's head. He defeated Satan on our behalf. All who put their faith in Jesus Christ share in His victory both now and forever.

Satan's defeat, however, doesn't mean that he's incapacitated. In fact, Satan is still all too active in this world. He's constantly scheming to distract us from our commitment to Christ. In Ephesians 6:11 Paul challenges us to, *"Put on the full armor of God so that you can take your stand against the devil's schemes."* God has given us, through Jesus Christ, everything we need to resist temptation and have victory over Satan day by day.

Satan was defeated at the cross. In a future day he'll be forever put out of reach of God's people and will suffer eternal judgment in hell. Revelation 20:10, looking into the future, says, *"And the devil, who deceived them, was thrown into the lake of burning sulfur, where the beast and the false prophet had been thrown. They will be tormented day and night forever and ever."* Satan's defeat is sealed. Jesus Christ has won the victory. Isn't it great to know that we're on the winning team!

DEMONS

• • • • • • • • •

When Jesus was on earth He frequently encountered people who were demon possessed. Sometimes their presence revealed itself in physical ways, such as inflicting blindness, prohibiting speech, or inciting erratic behavior. For example, Luke 9:38-39 tells us, *"A man in the crowd called out, 'Teacher, I beg you to look at my son, for he is my only child. A spirit seizes him and he suddenly screams; it throws him into convulsions so that he foams at the mouth.'"* Jesus healed many people of such demonic influence.

So, what are demons and are they real? The Bible presents demons as real spirit beings, not simply superstitious explanations for certain physical ailments. When God created the universe He created a class of spirit beings called angels. Some of those angels, under the leadership of Satan, rebelled against God and became the demons we read about in the Gospels. Revelation 12:7 tells us, *"And there was war in heaven. Michael and his angels fought against the dragon, and the dragon and his angels fought back."* God's holy angels stand in opposition to Satan and the fallen angels, or demons.

Because demons are spirit beings they have unusual powers. They can inflict diseases, reveal hidden secrets, and even possess individuals who open themselves to demonic activity. On one of his missionary journeys Paul encountered a girl who was possessed by a demon. Acts

16:16 says, *"Once when we were going to the place of prayer, we were met by a slave girl who had a spirit by which she predicted the future."* Paul cast the demon out of the girl in the name of Jesus. Because demons have such unusual powers, people are sometimes attracted to demonic influences. But the Bible forbids involving ourselves in such practices. Deuteronomy 18:10-11 says, *"Let no one be found among you who . . . practices divination or sorcery, interprets omens, engages in witchcraft, or casts spells, or who is a medium or spiritist or who consults the dead."* Demons are real and they're powerful. Christians should avoid any connection with demonic activity.

Although demons are powerful enemies of God's people, they're limited in what they can do and they face a certain doom. Jesus demonstrated His authority by casting out demons by His spoken word. In the future God will judge Satan and the demons, sending them to hell. Jesus, in Matthew 25:41, warned about future judgment, saying, *"Then he will say to those on his left, 'Depart from me, you who are cursed, into the eternal fire prepared for the devil and his angels.'"* When we receive Jesus as our Savior we enter into His protective power. Christians need never fear demonic powers because Jesus' power is greater. Doesn't it make sense to follow Jesus?

THE NATURE
OF HUMANITY

CREATED IN GOD'S IMAGE

· · · · · · · ·

It certainly presents an awkward moment for parents when their preschooler asks, "Where do babies come from?" But some Christians find it awkward to answer a bigger question in the face of our science-rich culture—"Where did man come from?" Are we the product of random evolutionary forces or are we the result of a creative act of God? The Bible doesn't hesitate, and neither should we, to identify our existence as the work of God. We were created in God's image.

Genesis 1:26 states, *"Then God said, 'Let us make man in our image, in our likeness.'"* Verse 27 goes on to say, *"So God created man in his own image, in the image of God he created him, male and female he created them."* God created human beings in His own image.

But what does it mean to be created in the image of God? It certainly doesn't mean that we bear a physical resemblance to God because God is pure spirit. So our resemblance to God must reside in our immaterial nature. We share both a moral and a personal likeness to God. Morally, the first man and woman were created both innocent and holy in character. There was no taint of sin in Adam and Eve. Genesis 1:31 tells us, *"God saw all that he had made, and it was very good."* This assessment by God included the moral condition of the first man and woman.

In addition to a moral likeness, God created us to have a personal likeness to Him. Personality includes three elements—intellect, emotion, and will. Like God we have a capacity to think, to feel, and to choose. This personal likeness to God makes us stand out from the rest of the physical creation. It gives us the ability to entertain abstract thoughts, to enjoy aesthetic wonders, and to engage in intentional worship of God.

Regrettably, sin entered the picture. While sin didn't erase the image of God in us, it did mar that image. Because we retain even a marred image of God, we're to treat one another with dignity and respect. James 3:9-10 says, *"With the tongue we praise our Lord and Father, and with it we curse men, who have been made in God's likeness. Out of the same mouth come praise and cursing. My brothers, this should not be."* Because we were made in God's image, human life and dignity are still sacred.

There's good news, however, about our fallen condition. God, through Jesus Christ, is restoring the fullness of His image in us. Ephesians 4:24 says that in Christ we are *"created to be like God in true righteousness and holiness."* Do you have Jesus in your heart? Invite Him to be your Savior today and welcome His transforming work in your life every day.

BODY, SOUL, AND SPIRIT

· · · · · · · ·

Amazingly, the human body consists of 206 different bones, over 20 internal organs, 600 distinct muscles, and trillions of microscopic cells. Our bodies are complex. But our bodies are only a part of our human makeup. The Bible says that we possess both material and immaterial parts. We each have a body, a soul, and a human spirit all wrapped up in a single, unified whole. In 1Thessalonians 5:24 Paul wrote, *"May your whole spirit, soul and body be kept blameless at the coming of our Lord Jesus Christ."* We are unique in God's creation.

There's some debate among theologians whether or not we're made up of two parts or three. In Matthew 10:28 Jesus, speaking of the total person, said, *"Do not be afraid of those who kill the body but cannot kill the soul."* On the other hand, Hebrews 4:12 tells us that the Word of God is *"sharper than any double-edge sword"* and *"penetrates even to dividing soul and spirit,"* indicating that the soul and the spirit are distinct. There's no simple answer to the question of how many parts compose an individual human being. In fact, Jesus said in Mark 12:30, *"Love the Lord your God with all your heart and with all your soul and with all your mind and with all your strength."* We can conclude that both our physical and spiritual components

Three-Minute Theology

form a complex unity. We each have a body, a soul, a spirit, a heart, a mind, and much more.

In simple terms we could say that our bodies make it possible for us to connect with the physical world, our souls connect us with ourselves and others around us, and our spirits connect us with God. We're physical, social, and spiritual beings. In addition, we possess the ability to think, to feel, and to choose. All of these aspects of our human makeup interact intricately. When our bodies hurt, we feel discouraged or even depressed. On the other hand, a joyful heart can help us overcome physical hardships. Proverbs 17:22 says, *"A cheerful heart is good medicine, but a crushed spirit dries up the bones."*

We are, indeed, complex beings. Psalm 139:14 beautifully expresses the mystery of our human makeup, saying, *"I praise you because I am fearfully and wonderfully made; your works are wonderful, I know that full well."* Because we're a work of our creative God there's a wonderful mystery about our human existence. Another aspect of that mystery is the fact that God has created us to live forever. Eternal life is available through faith in Jesus Christ alone. Romans 6:23 says, *"For the wages of sin is death, but the gift of God is eternal life in Christ Jesus our Lord."* God has created you in a miraculously wonderful way and He wants you to live with Him in heaven forever. Invite Jesus into your life today and you'll receive God's gift of eternal life.

THE FALL

· · · · · · · · ·

A little boy recently asked me, "Why did God create sin?" Of course, God didn't create sin. I explained that God is perfect, but Satan turned against God and thereby "created" sin. Eventually, people followed Satan's example and disobeyed God. Therefore, sin entered the human race. The first act of human sin is called the Fall. Adam and Eve disobeyed God and fell from perfect fellowship with Him. Everyone born since the Fall, apart from Jesus Christ, shares in that sin. The Fall has infected all of us. We're sinners by birth and sinners by choice.

Genesis 3:6-7 describes the tragic historical event called the Fall. *"When the woman saw that the fruit of the tree was good for food and pleasing to the eye, and also desirable for gaining wisdom, she took some and ate it. She also gave some to her husband, who was with her, and he ate it. Then the eyes of both of them were opened, and they realized they were naked; so they sewed fig leaves together and made coverings for themselves."* God had given Adam and Eve everything in the Garden of Eden for their enjoyment with the exception of one tree. In Genesis 2:17 God warned, *"But you must not eat from the tree of the knowledge of good and evil, for when you eat of it you will surely die."* At Satan's prompting, Eve disobeyed God's command as did Adam. Both immediately realized that something was terribly wrong and they tried to hide their shame. They tried to hide from God. But we can't hide from God. God soon confronted Adam and Eve with their sin. He also offered them hope.

The Fall had wide reaching consequences. The immediate effect of this first sin was spiritual death. Adam and Eve died that day, spiritually speaking. They were immediately cut off from God. This spiritual death could only be remedied through a spiritual rebirth based on faith in the gracious provision of God. Ultimately, Jesus would die for this and every other human sin in order to pave the way for restoration and salvation.

Furthermore, the Fall infected every descendant of Adam and Eve. First Corinthians 15:22 says, *"For as in Adam all die, so in Christ all will be made alive."* All of us are born spiritually dead because of our relationship with Adam, and that spiritual death will result in physical and even eternal death. But when we receive Jesus Christ, our sinless sacrifice for sin, we're made alive, alive spiritually and alive eternally.

Have you entered into the saving grace of Jesus Christ by faith? If not, why not stop right now and invite Jesus into your heart? If you have Jesus in your heart, you've passed from death to life. Isn't it great to know that our sins have been forgiven through Jesus Christ!

TEMPTATION

. . . .

Temptation is a word we use for various levels of undisciplined behavior. We may be tempted to hit the snooze button one too many times and arrive late at work. We're tempted to have a piece of chocolate cake instead of sticking with our diet. At a much more insidious level we're tempted every day to wander into sin against a holy God. We're tempted to lie, swear, lust, hate, lose our tempers, worry, gossip, complain, malign, and a host of other sins. Why is temptation so prevalent in our lives?

To begin with, we must understand that God never tempts us to sin. James 1:13 says, *"When tempted, no one should say, 'God is tempting me.' For God cannot be tempted by evil, nor does he tempt anyone."* So God is never the source of temptation, but we do have plenty of other sources of solicitation to evil. In simple terms we can say that temptation comes from three sources—the world, the flesh, and the devil.

The world wants us to follow its ungodly patterns. First John 2:16 says, *"For everything in the world— the cravings of sinful man, the lust of his eyes and the boasting of what he has and does—comes not from the Father but from the world."* Likewise, our inner, sinful being—our flesh—longs to sin. James 1:14 tells us, *"Each one is tempted when, by his own evil desire, he is dragged away and enticed."* Satan, too, tempts us to sin. First Peter 5:8 warns, *"Be self-controlled and alert. Your enemy the devil prowls around like a roaring lion looking for someone to devour."* The world, the flesh, and the devil each contribute to our daily temptations. But we can be victorious over temptation through the power of Jesus Christ.

The Bible tells us that God protects us from those temptations that would overwhelm us. In 1 Corinthians 10:13 we read, *"No temptation has seized you except what is common to man. And God is faithful; he will not let you be tempted beyond what you can bear. But when you are tempted he will provide a way out so that you can stand up under it."* Your particular temptations aren't unique. We're all tempted in many ways. Neither is your temptation unbearable. God has made a way of escape. We can resist temptation in the name of Jesus Christ our Savior. We do so by renewing our minds, replacing sinful patterns with healthy habits, and avoiding those situations in which temptation seems strongest.

First John 5:1-2 assures us of victory over temptation, saying, *"Everyone born of God overcomes the world. This is the victory that has overcome the world, even our faith. Who is it that overcomes the world? Only he who believes that Jesus is the Son of God."* Expect God to help you resist temptation today and thank Him for your victory in Jesus Christ.

SIN AND THE SIN NATURE

· · · · · · · ·

Sin is never a popular subject. Most people either deny that they sin or that their sins are of any real concern. Those who feel guilty over sin often resort to a try-harder remedy, hoping that their good intentions and extra efforts will in some way eclipse their failures. After all, won't God overlook our sins if we do enough good things? However, God's Word is clear about the consequences of even the least of sins. Romans 6:23 says, *"The wages of sin is death."* Because of our sins we're hopelessly lost unless God steps in.

As if that weren't bad enough, we learn from the Scriptures that sin takes on many forms in our lives. There are sins of commission and sins of omission; that is to say, we sin by actively disobeying God's commands and by passively neglecting to obey His will. James 2:10 tells us, *"For whoever keeps the whole law and yet stumbles at just one point is guilty of breaking it all,"* and James 4:17 states, *"Anyone, then, who knows the good he ought to do and doesn't do it, sins."* We can sin by our actions and by our inactions. We can even sin just by thinking evil thoughts. In Matthew 15:19 Jesus said, *"For out of the heart come evil thoughts, murder, adultery, sexual immorality, theft, false testimony, slander."* Sin is pervasive in our lives.

The reason sin is so strong in our lives is that we were born with a sinful nature. Galatians 5:16-17 tells us,

"Live by the Spirit, and you will not gratify the desires of the sinful nature. For the sinful nature desires what is contrary to the Spirit, and the Spirit what is contrary to the sinful nature. They are in conflict with each other, so that you do not do what you want." This sinful nature, the flesh, draws us away from God's holy standard. It entices us to act as sinners.

Simply stated, sin is any failure on our part to conform to God's holiness. Romans 3:23 says, *"For all have sinned and fall short of the glory of God."* No one measures up to God's glory. We're sinners by birth and by choice. Romans 5:12 tells us, *"Therefore, just as sin entered the world through one man, and death through sin, and in this way death came to all men, because all sinned."*

However, the Bible offers some very good news. Jesus took our sins on Himself so that we can be totally forgiven. Second Corinthians 5:21 declares, *"God made him who had no sin to be sin for us, so that in him we might become the righteousness of God."* Jesus died on the cross to pay the penalty for our sins. When we receive Jesus into our hearts by faith He forgives our sins and restores us to a right relationship with God. Thank God today for Jesus Christ and His loving sacrifice for your sins.

SUCH A GREAT SALVATION

SALVATION

• • • • • • • •

Imagine that you're in a little boat on a stormy sea. Suddenly you find yourself overboard, sinking quickly into the cold, murky water. You cry out in desperation, "Help, save me!" Then a hand reaches out of nowhere and rescues you. You have been, quite literally, saved! In fact, this is exactly the term that Peter used when he, having walked briefly on the Sea of Galilee, began to sink. According to Matthew 14:30, Peter cried out, *"Lord, save me!"* To be saved from physical danger or natural disaster would be an incredible life experience. Even greater is our opportunity to be saved from eternal spiritual death.

Our need for salvation is a constant theme in Scripture. Jesus, in John 3:17, said, *"For God did not send his Son into the world to condemn the world, but to save the world through him."* But what is salvation, and how can we know if we're truly saved in God's sight?

A helpful synonym for salvation is the word "deliverance." When we're saved, we've been delivered from a lost condition to a position of safety. Before we were saved, we were *"children of wrath,"* as Ephesians 2:3 puts it. This means that, because of our sin, we were under God's righteous anger and judgment. But Romans 5:9 says, *"Since we have now been justified by his blood, how much more shall we be saved from God's wrath through him!"* Through faith in Jesus Christ, we've been delivered from a position of God's disfavor to a position of His favor and blessing—right here, right now! Salvation isn't just a truth for the future. It applies to our present position as God's children.

However, salvation does change our future destination as well. Those who aren't saved have nothing but eternal judgment in hell waiting for them. But when we're saved, we're delivered from a future in hell to a future in heaven with God. Second Thessalonians 2:10 warns about a future without Jesus Christ, saying, *"They perish because they refused to love the truth and so be saved."* By contrast, in 2 Timothy 4:18 Paul expressed his confident faith that the Lord would deliver him *"to his heavenly kingdom."* Those who are saved have been delivered from a future in hell to a glorious future in heaven.

So what does it take to be saved? The good news is this—the work has already been done. Jesus died in your place on the cross. You need only receive Jesus into your heart by faith and you can be certain that you're saved. Ephesians 2:8 tells us, *"For it is by grace you have been saved through faith—and this not from yourselves, it is the gift of God."* Why not accept Jesus' free gift of salvation right now, and thank Him for delivering you from wrath and judgment to a position of favor and to a future in heaven?

ATONEMENT

• • • • • • • •

Imagine that you're throwing a big dinner party. Minutes before the guests begin to arrive, you accidentally spill a glass of grape juice on your beautiful white carpet. There's no time to remove the stain. You'll have to improvise. Your solution to the problem is to cover the stain with a throw rug until after the party, when you can remove the stain entirely.

The Bible uses a word for covering a stain. It's the word "atonement." Each one of us has a stained heart. Our sins have left their mark. We'd like to cover up our sins so that no one, especially God, sees them. In fact, people are constantly trying to hide their sins. But we can't really keep God from seeing our hearts.

Thankfully, God has a remedy for our sins. In Old Testament times, God had instructed His people to bring animal sacrifices to the Temple. The high priest would take the blood of a sacrificial animal and apply it to the mercy seat on the Ark of the Covenant. The blood would cover over Israel's sins. Leviticus 16:15 says, *"In this way he will make atonement for the Most Holy Place because of the uncleanness and rebellion of the Israelites, whatever their sins have been."* The idea behind this practice was that God would no longer see the people's sins and would therefore maintain fellowship with them. The word "atone" literally means "at one." Through the atonement we are at one with God in fellowship and relationship.

However, like the throw rug covering the grape juice stain until after the party, the animal sacrifices were only a temporary measure. Jesus died on the cross to atone for our sins. But He didn't simply cover them up. He washed them away. John the Baptist, in John 1:29, said, *"Look, the Lamb of God, who takes away the sin of the world."* Jesus doesn't merely cover our sins. He washes them away. By His atoning death we can be at one with God.

There is some debate among Christians as to the extent of Christ's atoning work. Some suggest that the benefits of Jesus' death are limited, that Jesus died only for those who would eventually come to Him by faith. Others think that Jesus died for everyone, that His atonement is unlimited. First Timothy 4:10 tips the scale in favor of an unlimited atonement in my thinking. It says, *"We have put our hope in the living God, who is the Savior of all men, and especially of those who believe."* This doesn't mean that everyone *will* be saved, but that everyone *can* be saved.

But no matter what you believe about the extent of Christ's atonement, we can all agree that without His death on the cross we couldn't be saved. We need Jesus to remove the stain of sin in our hearts. Have you received Jesus as your Savior? Ask Him to come into your life. He's eager to completely wash your sins away.

REDEMPTION

· · · · · · · ·

I once read a story about a little boy who built a toy boat. He drew up the plans, cut out the wood, assembled the craft, and painted it so that it was a beautiful little vessel. The boy then tied a string to the boat and launched it into the nearby stream. Unfortunately, the string broke and the current took the little boat away. The boy, of course, was heartbroken. A few days later that same little boy went into a toy shop and, much to his surprise, he saw his boat on a shelf with a price tag on it. The boy eagerly paid the price to retrieve his precious boat. The boat was, in a way, twice his—once by creation and once by purchase.

This story illustrates the biblical concept of "redemption." We belong to God by creation. He made us. Yet our sins have carried us far away from Him. In order to bring us back into His fellowship, God paid a price. That price was the death of His Son, Jesus Christ. First Peter 1:18-19 says, *"For you know that it was not with perishable things such as silver or gold that you were redeemed from the empty way of life handed down to you from your forefathers, but with the precious blood of Christ."*

Redemption actually involves two distinct ideas. One aspect of redemption is that of making a purchase. The New Testament uses a word that was common in ancient Rome for purchasing and releasing a slave. For example, 1 Corinthians 7:23 tells us, *"You were bought at a price; do not become slaves of men."* Human slavery is, of course, an abominable practice. Even more tragic is our slavery to sin. But Jesus Christ paid the price to free us from the power of sin and death. He redeemed us.

Another aspect of our redemption has to do with the idea of paying a ransom. Sin holds us hostage. But Jesus Christ paid the ransom price so that we could be restored to fellowship with God. First Timothy 2:5-6 says, *"For there is one God and one mediator between God and men, the man Christ Jesus, who gave himself as a ransom for all men."* God's divine justice was satisfied by Jesus' death on the cross. Jesus ransomed us from our captivity to sin.

Of course, we enter into the benefits of Jesus' redeeming work only when we receive Jesus Christ into our hearts by faith. Romans 3:22-24 puts faith and redemption together, saying, *"This righteousness from God comes through faith in Jesus Christ to all who believe. There is no difference, for all have sinned and fall short of the glory of God, and are justified freely by his grace through the redemption that came by Christ Jesus."* Have you entered into the blessing of Christ's redemption? He offers you freedom and forgiveness. Why not invite Jesus into your life today?

PROPITIATION

· · · · · · · · ·

Human relationships are fragile. Husbands and wives sometimes find themselves at odds with each other, often over trivial issues. Friendships can become strained because of insensitive words or actions. When we experience a seemingly irreparable rift in a relationship, we welcome the intercession of an outside party—a counselor, a family member, or another friend—who can help bring us back into harmony.

Our relationship with God is much like a broken relationship with a loved one. God loves us, but because we sinned against Him our relationship is severed. Isaiah 59:2 says, *"Your iniquities have separated you from your God; your sins have hidden his face from you, so that he will not hear."* Not only is our relationship with God broken due to sin, but according to Romans 5:10 we find ourselves in the position of being *"God's enemies."* Therefore, we are objects of God's wrath—His righteous anger and judgment. If only someone could intercede for us. If only someone could remove God's anger and restore us to a healthy relationship with Him. In fact, that someone is Jesus Christ.

By His death on the cross Jesus removed the barrier that stood between us and God. He perfectly satisfied God's holy justice. To use a theological term, Jesus "propitiated" God. Propitiation refers to the removal of God's righteous wrath caused by our sins. It's as if God had to turn His back on us when we sinned, but now can turn toward us

Three-Minute Theology

with outstretched arms once again. Luke 18:13 records one of Jesus' parables in which a penitent tax collector cried out, *"God, have mercy on me, a sinner."* The word "mercy" reflects the term for "propitiation." That poor man was calling out to God for mercy. He wanted God to receive him, sinner that he was, with outstretched arms.

God the Father can indeed turn toward us in mercy because Jesus Christ removed our sins. He is our propitiation, also translated as our atoning sacrifice. First John 2:2 tells us, *"He is the atoning sacrifice for our sins,"* and 1 John 4:10 goes on to say, *"This is love: not that we loved God, but that he loved us and sent his Son as an atoning sacrifice for our sins."* These verses remind us that even though we were objects of God's righteous anger, we never stopped being objects of His love. Because He loves us, He sent Jesus to remove the barrier that was between us. He has been propitiated. He is satisfied with Jesus' death. Furthermore, when we have Jesus in our lives, God the Father is satisfied with us.

Do you have Jesus in your life? He died to bring you back into fellowship with God. Why not accept Him by faith today? You'll find that God awaits you with outstretched arms!

SUBSTITUTION

∙ ∙ ∙ ∙ ∙ ∙ ∙ ∙

When a player is injured on the football field or the basketball court, the coach sends in a substitute, a healthy player who can take the place of the injured teammate. In the spiritual realm we need a substitute. We've been injured by sin, unable to participate in spiritual life with God. Even worse, our sin demands death, separation from God for all eternity. Thankfully, Jesus Christ came into this world to be our substitute. He took our place by dying on the cross.

The concept of "substitution" is foundational to the Christian faith. Because of the substitutionary atonement of Jesus Christ we can experience the complete forgiveness of our sins.

Substitution first appears in the Old Testament sacrificial system. According to the ceremonial laws, if a man sinned he was to find an unblemished goat for a sin offering. Leviticus 4:27 says, *"He is to lay his hand on the head of the sin offering and slaughter it at the place of the burnt offering."* Laying hands on the animal symbolized a transfer of sin and guilt to the sacrificial animal. After the animal was slaughtered, a priest was to apply its blood to the altar. Leviticus 4:35 goes on to say, *"In this way the priest will make atonement for him for the sin he has committed, and he will be forgiven."* The animal served as a substitute for the man's sins.

We don't have to sacrifice animals on an altar today in order to receive forgiveness. God has provided a better way. His Son, Jesus Christ, became our perfect substitute for sin. Isaiah 53:5-6 says, *"But he was pierced for our transgressions, he was crushed for our iniquities; the punishment that brought us peace was upon him, and by his wounds we are healed. We all, like sheep, have gone astray, each of us has turned to his own way; and the Lord has laid on him the iniquity of us all."* Jesus took our punishment by dying in our place.

The New Testament underscores the doctrine of Christ's substitutionary atonement. It reminds us that Jesus Christ died "for" us. Jesus, in John 10:11, said, *"I am the good shepherd. The good shepherd lays down his life for the sheep."* Romans 5:8 tells us, *"While we were still sinners, Christ died for us."* First Peter 3:18 says, *"For Christ died for sins once for all, the righteous for the unrighteous, to bring you to God."* Clearly, Jesus became our substitute. Just try to imagine how horrible it would have been if you had been crucified on that cross. Instead, Jesus died for you.

Because Jesus died in your place, you can experience His forgiveness and receive eternal life. Don't miss out on the greatest gift you'll ever receive. Invite Jesus into your heart, and thank Him for being your substitute.

YOUR POSITION IN CHRIST

JUSTIFICATION

....

Wouldn't it be great if we could be sure that we're right with God? Let's face it. Every one of us has doubts about our standing with God. Can God look at us with favor, or are we hopelessly trapped in a lifelong process of trying to please and appease a holy God? Thankfully, God's Word assures us that we can be right with God—right here, right now, right with God.

First of all, we need to understand that we can do nothing to contribute to a right standing in God's sight. We have to depend on God to do that for us. Because we're sinners both by birth and by choice, we need God to step in and change our situation. We need Him to declare us right in His sight. The idea that God would declare us right according to His holy standard is called "justification." Only God can declare us right in His sight, legally and eternally righteous. Romans 8:33 says, *"It is God who justifies."*

Justification is the opposite of condemnation. In our sin, we're objects of God's condemning judgment. But in Christ, we move from a position of condemnation to a position of justification. In Romans 5:16 we read, *"The gift of God is not like the result of the one man's sin: The judgment followed one sin and brought condemnation, but the gift followed many trespasses and brought justification."* In other words, Adam's one sin has passed down through the generations to every one of us, and we're born into a position of judgment. But Jesus Christ, through His death on the cross, paid for every sin. Therefore, He offers us the free gift of justification—God's declaration of our forgiveness and righteousness in His sight.

So, we might ask, what do we have to do to get this gift of justification? The point is, it's a gift. We can't earn gifts. We can only receive them. Many people have mistakenly thought that they could in some way earn God's favor. They've tried to "buy" God's grace by obeying a set of laws or performing acts of kindness to others. While these are good things, they won't make us right in God's eyes. No, we can receive the gift of justification only through faith in Jesus Christ. We have to believe that He is God, that He died in our place, and that He can really save us. The apostle Paul, in Galatians 2:16, said that we are not *"justified by observing the law, but by faith in Jesus Christ . . . ."* Later, in verse 21, he said, *"If righteousness could be gained through the law, Christ died for nothing!"* But Jesus Christ didn't die in vain. He died for us. We can't be declared right before God on our own merit. We need Jesus. Do you have Jesus? If so, you've been declared right with God. You've been justified by Him. If you don't have Jesus, why not invite Him into your heart right now. Then you, too, can be confident that you're right here, right now, right with God.

SANCTIFICATION

· · · · · · · ·

If you're the parent of an energetic preschooler, you know how much effort it takes to keep that little guy clean. You may start him out with a daily bath, but then throughout the day you have to wipe the food, dirt, goo, and other sticky stuff from his face, his hands, his clothes, and everything he touches. An initial bath is necessary, but there's also an ongoing need for cleansing. That's what takes place at the spiritual level as well. We call it "sanctification." At the moment you invited Jesus into your heart you were sanctified. But you also need to be sanctified over and over again as a result of your daily sins. Let's think about these two aspects of sanctification for a moment.

To be sanctified means to be set apart by God as holy in His sight. It's related to the term "saint," a holy person, a person who's been set apart from sin to live for God. By the way, the New Testament refers to all true believers as saints in this sense. Through faith in Jesus Christ, we're sanctified, made into saints in God's book.

When you asked Jesus to be your Savior, you were instantly sanctified. Your position of acceptance by God was established. The apostle Paul, having described some of the sinful lifestyles of the people of his day, wrote in 1 Corinthians 6:11, *"And that is what some of you were. But you were washed, you were sanctified, you were justified in the name of the Lord Jesus Christ and by the Spirit of our God."* This refers to a past, settled event in the life of the Christian. Have you accepted Jesus as your Savior? Then you have been positionally sanctified, set apart by God from your old sinful lifestyle to a new way of life in Christ.

But here's the rub. We don't always act so holy. Even as Christians, we fail to measure up to God's holy standard in the way we live our lives. So, having received our initial cleansing, we need to have our faces wiped over and over again. We need to be sanctified daily, hourly, even moment by moment. This progressive aspect of sanctification means that we, by God's grace, need to live in growing obedience to His holy standard. First Peter 1:15 says, *"But just as he who called you is holy, so be holy in all you do."* In other words, act in accordance with your position. Live a holy lifestyle because you're a holy person in God's eyes.

But how can we live holy lives? Only by the power of God at work in us. First Thessalonians 5:23 says, *"May God himself, the God of peace, sanctify you through and through."* When we accepted Jesus, we entered immediately into a sanctified position with God. Now, we need to live up to that position, setting ourselves apart from sin daily to live in harmony with God's holiness.

Invite Jesus into your heart today, and then begin living for Him.

GLORIFICATION

For Christians, there's much more to life than what this present world has to offer. Don't get me wrong. God has given us plenty of good things to enjoy here and now. While this world has its trials, it also has some amazing blessings.

Even so, we as Christians always keep one eye on heaven. We know that the best is yet to come. We look forward to a future transformation of our minds, hearts, and bodies that the Bible refers to as "glorification." Glorification means that we will one day experience totally all the benefits we now have in Jesus Christ positionally.

Let me put it this way. Glorification means that one day we're going to have a physical transformation. Our bodies are going to be reconfigured to enjoy eternity. We'll be free from physical suffering and pain. For those whose lives have been characterized by illnesses, limitations, and hardship the doctrine of glorification is a beacon of hope. Paul, in Romans 8:18, said, *"I consider that our present sufferings are not worth comparing with the glory that will be revealed in us."* Think about it—no more pain, no more suffering, no more diseases or illnesses or surgeries or chemo treatments. Our bodies will be glorified, transformed to be like the body of our resurrected Lord Jesus Christ. In Philippians 3:21, Paul says that Jesus Christ *"will transform our lowly bodies so that they will be like his glorious body."* We'll be free from suffering, free to enjoy heaven for all eternity.

But glorification doesn't refer only to the body. It refers to a spiritual transformation as well. In heaven our bodies will be free from suffering, and in heaven our spirits will be free from sin. First John 3:2 tells us, *"Dear friends, now we are children of God, and what we will be has not yet been made known. But we know that when he appears, we shall be like him, for we shall see him as he is."* Our minds can't begin to grasp the splendor of heaven or of our future glorified state. Right now our hearts are saturated with sin. We can barely imagine being free from sinful thoughts, motives, or attitudes. But in heaven we'll be like Jesus. We'll be free from the grip of sin, free from the emotional scars that leave a trail of sorrow in our lives, free from the persistent pestering of our sinful natures. We'll be able to entertain pure thoughts. We'll be able to enjoy pure relationships. We'll be transformed to live in holiness forever.

Have you received Jesus Christ as your Savior? If you have, God's Word assures you that you will one day be glorified. Why not invite Jesus into your heart right now? Then, let's enjoy the life God's given us here on earth, and let's look forward to the life God's promised us in heaven.

REGENERATION

· · · · · · · · ·

One of the many great things that happens to us when we receive Jesus Christ as our Savior is that we're granted lasting spiritual life. The Bible tells us that, without Jesus in our lives, we're spiritually dead. In John 5:24 Jesus said, *"I tell you the truth, whoever hears my word and believes him who sent me has eternal life and will not be condemned; he has crossed over from death to life."* As odd as it sounds, we begin life spiritually dead. But when we invite Jesus into our hearts we become spiritually alive. This act of God by which He grants us spiritual life is called "regeneration."

Regeneration is more commonly known as being born again, or experiencing a spiritual rebirth. Jesus once told a curious man named Nicodemus that, in order to get into heaven, he would have to be spiritually reborn. John 3:3 records Jesus' conversation, saying, *"I tell you the truth, no one can see the kingdom of God unless he is born again."* Regeneration is essential if we're going to go to heaven. We must be born again. We must have spiritual life.

But how do we get that spiritual life? How does regeneration work? To begin with, we know that there's nothing we can contribute to regeneration. We were born spiritually dead, remember? Being spiritually dead, we can't perform any spiritual act that will bring about a spiritual resuscitation. Regeneration must be an act of God, a gift that He gives us. After all, only God can create life, including spiritual life. Paul put it this way in Ephesians 2:4-5. *"But because of his great love for us, God, who is rich in mercy, made us alive with Christ even when we were dead in transgressions—it is by grace you have been saved."* So regeneration—being made spiritually alive—is an act of God prompted by His grace.

Even so, not everyone receives this gift of spiritual life. Regeneration is linked with our faith response to the work of Jesus Christ on the cross. John 1:12-13 says, *"Yet to all who received him, to those who believed in his name, he gave the right to become children of God—children born not of natural descent, nor of human decision or a husband's will, but born of God."* We're born again when we receive Jesus Christ. When we believe in Him, that is, when we put our faith in Him, He grants us new, eternal, spiritual life through an act of regeneration. We become alive for the first time in our lives! Our new life is far better than anything we could have experienced apart from Jesus Christ. That's why Jesus said, in John 10:10, *"I have come that they may have life, and have it to the full."*

Let me invite you to receive Jesus Christ by faith right now. Then you, too, can have this new, lasting, abundant spiritual life.

RECONCILIATION

· · · · · · · ·

Some of our greatest joys as well as some of our greatest struggles in life flow from our relationships with others. A happy marriage is a priceless treasure. Harmony in the home is golden. Quality friendships sharpen our lives. But when a marriage hits hard times, relational problems become all-consuming. When our kids get into serious trouble or grow rebellious in their attitudes, harmony in the home becomes a distant memory. When friendships falter, loneliness and isolation prevail. Healthy relationships bring us immeasurable joy, but broken relationships can scar us for life.

God wants to have a relationship with you. He wants to be your friend, your Father, your husband. The Bible uses these and other relational terms to describe God's connection with His people. When we're right with God, that spiritual relationship is unparalleled. Unfortunately, our sins have ruined our relationship with God. Instead of being His friend, we're His enemy. We're like rebellious children, or an unfaithful wife. Even if we wanted to return to God, we've built an immovable wall between Him and us. We need help.

When relationships fail, we try to restore them through a process called "reconciliation." A husband and wife who've mistreated each other need to be reconciled, brought back into an accepting and loving relationship. In the same way, we need to be reconciled to God. We need to be restored to a harmonious, loving relationship with

Him. In 2 Corinthians 5:20, Paul wrote, *"We implore you on Christ's behalf: Be reconciled to God."* Our relationship with God was ruined by sin. We actually act as enemies of God when we sin against Him. But God doesn't want us to be His enemy. He wants us to be His friend. So He urges us to be reconciled to Him.

But how can we be reconciled to God? As with other aspects of our salvation, we can't earn reconciliation. We can't force our way into God's favor by trying to do lots of good things. No, we need to depend totally on God's grace which He offers us through Jesus Christ. It's only through the sacrificial death of Jesus Christ on the cross that we can be reconciled to God. Romans 5:10 tells us, *"For if, when we were God's enemies, we were reconciled to him through the death of his Son, how much more, having been reconciled, shall we be saved through his life!"* Reconciliation with God is possible only through faith in Jesus Christ. Have you put your faith in Jesus Christ? Why not ask Him into your heart today?

Once we've been reconciled to God through faith in Jesus Christ, we'll find it much easier to be reconciled to other people. Broken relationships are hard to mend, but with Jesus Christ all things are possible.

ADOPTION

· · · · · · · · ·

We all know families who've adopted a child into their homes. I admire these families. We have several adoptive families in our church, and they, along with their adopted children, bring a richness to the body of Christ. Each has a special story to tell. Adoption is a wonderful, voluntary, sacrificial act of acceptance and love.

The Bible tells us that everyone who's accepted Jesus Christ as Savior has been adopted into the family of God. We've experienced spiritual adoption. Ephesians 1:5 tells us that we've been *"adopted as his sons through Jesus Christ, in accordance with his pleasure and will."* It pleases God to make us a part of His family. He wants us to experience His love and acceptance.

But spiritual adoption has more to it than simply being accepted by God. It also implies growth toward spiritual maturity. In ancient times a wealthy Roman family could adopt an adult son, granting that individual all the rights and freedoms that that family possessed. Adoption, in that setting, referred to recognizing maturity and bestowing the rights of maturity on a member of the family. We actually become a part of God's family through the new birth. Through adoption we're granted the rights and privileges of mature members of that family.

One special privilege that we receive through adoption is the right to call God our Father. In fact, we can speak to Him openly, in very intimate terms. In Romans 8:15

we read, *"For you did not receive a spirit that makes you a slave again to fear, but you received the Spirit of adoption. And by him we cry, 'Abba, Father.'"* Abba was an intimate term of affection that a child would use to refer to his or her own father. Because we are children of God by faith in Jesus Christ, we can call God our Father. We can pray to Him and be confident that He hears and answers our prayers.

Another privilege we receive through spiritual adoption into God's family is the blessing of participating in a spiritual inheritance with Jesus Christ in heaven. Galatians 4:6-7 says, *"Because you are sons, God sent the Spirit of his Son into our hearts, the Spirit who calls out 'Abba, Father.' So you are no longer a slave, but a son; and since you are a son, God has made you also an heir."* We inherit the riches of heaven because we've been adopted into God's family. We become *"heirs of God and co-heirs with Christ"* according to Romans 8:17. Because of our spiritual adoption, we can look forward to a day when we'll share in the joys of Jesus in heaven.

Think about it. You can be a member of God's family. You can be adopted by the Creator of the universe. You can become an heir to all that heaven has to offer. You need simply put your faith in Jesus Christ. Why not join God's family today? Then you can begin to grow into spiritual maturity as an adopted child of God.

SEVEN SNAPSHOTS OF THE LOCAL CHURCH

THE CHURCH AS A BODY

....

We've all heard someone say, "I don't need the church. I can be just as good a Christian at home." Worse yet, maybe you've found yourself thinking this from time to time. While it's true that we can pray at home, study the Scriptures at home, and worship God at home, there are aspects of our Christian life that must take place in the context of Christians gathered together in community. We need the church, and the church needs us.

The Bible describes the church as a "body." The human body needs every member, every part, every organ, to work effectively. The apostle Paul put it this way in 1 Corinthians 12:12. *"The body is a unit, though it is made up of many parts; and though all its parts are many, they form one body. So it is with Christ."* Christians form a body. We're spiritually connected with one another and with Jesus Christ.

Because the church is like our physical bodies, we should expect that there will be diversity within the body. Think about it. Our physical bodies consist of dozens and dozens of different parts. We have hands, feet, eyes, ears, a heart, a tongue, a skeletal structure—the list goes on and on. Each part plays an essential role in the body.

Likewise, the church is a body of diverse people. God delights in racial diversity in the church. He's called people from every tongue and tribe and nation to be a part of His church. God delights in age diversity. Children and teens should be equally at home in the church with young adults, middle-agers, and seniors. A church with a diversity of ages is balanced and vibrant. God delights in the diversity of personalities in the church. Some of God's people are quiet and analytical. Some are loud and energetic. Others are emotional, or intellectual, or relational, or even practical. God also delights in the diversity of gifts—spiritual abilities—in the church. Some teach, some serve, some lead, some organize, some show mercy, some have a special knack for sharing their faith or giving generously of their resources. All are valuable to God.

There's one more thing we need to understand about the church as a body. The body needs a head. Jesus Christ, the Son of God, is that Head. Ephesians 4:15-16 says, *"Instead, speaking the truth in love, we will in all things grow up into him who is the Head, that is, Christ. From him the whole body, joined and held together by every supporting ligament, grows and builds itself up in love, as each part does its work."* Jesus is our Head. By His grace He joins us together, holds us together, and directs our steps.

Every church is responsible for looking to Jesus for its direction. Every Christian is responsible for honoring Jesus in his or her life. In order to honor Him, we must honor His body—the church. We need Jesus and, according to Jesus, we need each other.

THE CHURCH AS A BUILDING

· · · · · · · ·

When you hear the word "church," what's the first image that comes to your mind? Is it a white clapboard building with stained glass windows and a tall, pointed steeple? Of course, a church is not a building. The church is people. But you'll find it interesting to know that the New Testament sometimes describes the church as a building, a holy temple that brings glory to the Lord Jesus Christ.

For example, Ephesians 2:21-22 says that in Christ *"the whole building is joined together and rises to become a holy temple in the Lord."* In 1 Peter 2:5 we read, *"You also, like living stones, are being built into a spiritual house."* Each and every Christian is a part of the church, a building block in a great and glorious temple for God. We are "living stones." As such, Jesus Christ is carefully shaping us to fit neatly into His temple. With His loving hands He's chiseling off the rough places in our lives. As a master craftsman, Jesus places us in strategic relationship with the rest of His people in such a way that we form interlocking connections with one another. His work of spiritual construction guarantees that the church will have incredible, enduring strength. In Matthew 16:18 Jesus told His disciples, *"I will build my church, and the gates of Hell will not overcome it."* As a solid edifice, built stone by stone by the magnificent skill of Jesus Christ, the church forms an unconquerable fortress. You and I, as living stones, are a part of that structure. Through faith in Jesus Christ, our lives add to the strength and beauty of the church. That's why it's so important that we live holy lives day in and day out. We're part of a holy temple, a spiritual house—the church.

There's really only one reason that the church has such enduring strength. Jesus Christ is our strength. We've already seen that Jesus is building His church. But the New Testament also tells us that Jesus is the very foundation of the church. Any building that's going to withstand the forces of time and nature needs to have a solid foundation. We, as living stones within the church, have Jesus Christ as our foundation. First Corinthians 3:11 says, *"For no one can lay any foundation other than the one already laid, which is Jesus Christ."* Our strength rests in our relationship with Jesus. He is unshakable! When you think that the difficulties in your life are going to overwhelm you, remember that Jesus is your foundation. He'll see you through any storm. He'll sustain you through any earthquake that shakes your life.

So the church consists of people, not bricks and boards and shingles. But like a building, the church has a solid foundation and a skillful master builder—Jesus Christ.

THE CHURCH AS A BRIDE

· · · · · · · ·

Wedding bells are a delight to every young bride. Her day at last has arrived! The guests are seated. The bridesmaids are lined up in their beautiful dresses. The groom and his groomsmen stand ready for the ceremony. The flowers, the photographer, the minister—everything is in place. The bride—beaming and beautiful in her wedding gown—is escorted up the aisle to join in lifelong union with her beloved. It's a day that will last forever in her heart.

The image of a bride, prepared for her wedding day, provides us with one of the most beautiful snapshots of the church. Revelation 19:7-8 says, *"Let us rejoice and be glad and give him glory! For the wedding of the Lamb has come, and his bride has made herself ready. Fine linen, bright and clean, was given her to wear."* And then verse 8 goes on to explain, *"Fine linen stands for the righteous acts of the saints."* According to the New Testament, all true believers in Jesus Christ are saints, that is, people who have been set apart as holy in God's sight through the gracious sacrifice of Jesus on the cross. As saints, we have been spiritually clothed in pure, white, fine linen. In other words, our hearts and lives have been purified. Our sins have been washed away. We appear spotless in the eyes of God. Like a bride in her radiant white wedding gown, we enter into the presence of our Lord Jesus Christ as pure, holy, and beautiful in His sight. We, the church, are the bride of Christ.

As the bride of Jesus Christ, we want to live up to our privileged relationship. We want to be pure in our practical living, just as we've been made pure and holy in our position in Christ. Paul put it this way in 2 Corinthians 11:2. *"I promised you to one husband, to Christ, so that I might present you as a pure virgin to him."* When we enter into the presence of Jesus Christ, we want to present Him with a wedding gift, a life of purity and faithfulness. This is the goal of every true believer. This is likewise the goal of each and every local church.

Isn't it great to know that we have someone who loves us? Because we are His bride, Jesus Christ loves us unconditionally. He demonstrated that love for us by dying for our sins on the cross. Ephesians 5:25-27 says, *"Husbands, love your wives just as Christ loved the church and gave himself up for her to make her holy, cleansing her by the washing with water through the word, and to present her to himself as a radiant church, without stain or wrinkle or any other blemish, but holy and blameless."* Jesus loves us. He died for us. He purifies us. And one day He's coming back to take us into His loving presence forever. We are the bride of Jesus Christ. He's our loving groom and our gracious Savior. Let the wedding bells ring!

THE CHURCH AS A FAMILY

....

Relationships are essential for a healthy church. Christians need to see themselves as living in a vital relationship with one another and in a vibrant relationship with Jesus Christ. Because relationships are so important, the New Testament sometimes describes the church as a spiritual family.

Galatians 6:10 says, *"Therefore, as we have opportunity, let us do good to all people, especially to those who belong to the family of believers,"* or *"household of faith."* Through the new birth we've entered a new family, the family of God—the church. We're spiritually related to every other believer, past, present, and future. We're part of an amazing family tree! Some of our family members have endured great hardship for the sake of Jesus Christ. They've been persecuted, tortured, and even killed just for being a part of the family. Others, by God's grace, have accomplished great things in the fields of science, medicine, education, literature, politics, and business. We have an amazing family.

The New Testament frequently describes Christians as brothers and sisters. For example, Hebrews 13:1 says, *"Keep on loving each other as brothers."* First Peter 3:8 tells us, *"Finally, all of you, live in harmony with one another; be sympathetic, love as brothers, be compassionate and humble."* First Timothy 5:1-2 says,

"Do not rebuke an older man harshly, but exhort him as if he were your father. Treat younger men as brothers, older women as mothers, and younger women as sisters, with absolute purity." These references remind us that we must treat our brothers and sisters with love, respect, and generosity. We're to get along with them in unity and humility.

In addition to nurturing proper attitudes toward our church family, we're to act as responsible family members. In 1 Timothy 3:15-16, Paul says that he expects us to *"know how people ought to conduct themselves in God's household, which is the church of the living God, the pillar and foundation of the truth."* We're responsible to encourage one another, support one another, serve one another, and love one another.

So how does Jesus Christ fit into this image of the church as a family? Jesus described Himself as our Brother. In Mark 3:35 He says, *"Whoever does God's will is my brother and sister and mother."* Hebrews 2:11 reinforces this idea, saying, *"Both the one who makes men holy and those who are made holy are of the same family. So Jesus is not ashamed to call them brothers."* Jesus is our Brother, made like us through the incarnation and related to us through our new birth. Through faith in Jesus Christ we become a part of God's spiritual family, the church. Isn't it great to be a part of the family of God!

THE CHURCH AS A FLOCK

· · · · · · · ·

Sheep and their shepherds were common sights in ancient Bible lands. Even today, you can see shepherds in the fields of Israel. No wonder the image of a flock of sheep became a picture of the church.

In the tenth chapter of John's Gospel, Jesus describes His people as sheep, humble creatures in need of a loving, faithful shepherd. In verse 14 Jesus says, *"I am the good shepherd; I know my sheep and my sheep know me."* In verse 16, He says *"I have other sheep that are not of this sheep pen. I must bring them also. They too will listen to my voice, and there shall be one flock and one shepherd."*

Through His death on the cross—as the spotless Lamb of God—Jesus made it possible for us to enter into His flock by faith. In fact, Jesus invites us to listen to His voice and follow Him. However, like sheep we tend to wander from the protective fold of our shepherd. Isaiah 53:6 reminds us, *"We all, like sheep, have gone astray, each of us has turned to his own way; and the Lord has laid on him the iniquity of us all."* Our sinful human nature prompts us to launch out on our own, to become distant from our shepherd, and to try to be independent from the flock. But Jesus invites us back to His protective, loving care. When we put our faith in Jesus, He guides us into the fellowship of other sheep. He unites us as a flock, His church.

Within the church, Jesus Christ has appointed certain individuals to serve as shepherds for His flock. Another word for shepherd is "pastor." Pastors have been called by God to protect and lead the church. In Acts 20:28, Paul told pastors, *"Keep watch over yourselves and all the flock of which the Holy Spirit has made you overseers. Be shepherds of the church of God, which he bought with his own blood."* Pastors have a high calling, a humble position, and a huge responsibility as shepherds of Christ's church.

Ultimately, however, Jesus Christ Himself is the Shepherd of the church. In John 10:11, Jesus says, *"I am the good shepherd. The good shepherd lays down his life for the sheep."* Jesus gave His life on the cross in order to save us from the deadliest enemy, death itself. Hebrews 13:20 describes the resurrected Jesus as *"that great Shepherd of the sheep."* First Peter 5:4 tells us, *"And when the Chief Shepherd appears, you will receive the crown of glory that will never fade away."* Jesus is the good Shepherd, the great Shepherd, and the chief Shepherd. He died for the flock. He rose from the dead for the sake of the flock. He rewards His flock with eternal glory. The church is a flock, humble sheep under the care of the most loving Shepherd. With the writer of Psalm 23:1, we can say with confidence, *"The Lord is my shepherd."*

THE CHURCH AS A GRAPEVINE

· · · · · · · ·

In John 15:5 Jesus says, *"I am the vine; you are the branches. If a man remains in me and I in him, he will bear much fruit; apart from me you can do nothing."* With this statement, Jesus portrays the church as a grapevine with each branch, each Christian, intimately dependent on Him.

The goal of any vineyard owner is to produce as much quality fruit as possible. In order to produce any fruit, the branches must not be severed from the vine. And in order to produce a bountiful harvest, each branch needs to be carefully pruned.

Jesus used this image of the grapevine to teach us how important it is for us to stay in close fellowship with Him. As Christians, we far too easily drift away from Christ in our day to day routines. We rush off to school or work without taking time to read from God's Word. We hurry through our prayers or, even worse, fail to pray altogether. We rarely take time to reflect on Jesus and our relationship with Him. But without these connecting points in our lives, we'll never be able to produce quality spiritual fruit. Jesus put it this way in John 15:4. *"Abide in me, and I will abide in you. No branch can bear fruit by itself; it must abide in the vine. Neither can you bear fruit unless you abide in me."* Abiding in Jesus means that we need to have unhurried, lingering fellowship with Him. We need to meditate on His Word and pray for His direction. We need to acknowledge day by day and moment by moment our dependence on Jesus.

But Jesus isn't simply interested in our fellowship with Him. He wants us to bear fruit—not some fruit, but much fruit. For this reason Jesus allows us to go through times of pruning. God the Father, as the vinedresser, lovingly cuts away those things in our lives that prohibit spiritual fruit. In John 15:2 Jesus says, *"He cuts off every branch in me that bears no fruit, while every branch that does bear fruit he prunes so that it will be even more fruitful."* God wants His people, His church, to be spiritually productive in this world. At times we go through trials, the pruning work of God in our lives, so that we can become even more fruitful.

As the vine, Jesus Christ is the source of our life, our nourishment, and our support. When we put our faith in Him, He lifts us up, feeds our hearts, and helps us to have a truly fruitful life. How close are you to Jesus Christ? One way to measure the fruit in your life is to reflect on Galatians 5:22-23. *"But the fruit of the Spirit is love, joy, peace, patience, kindness, goodness, faithfulness, gentleness, and self control."* Jesus wants to produce this kind of fruit in your life and in the church. So, keep connected to the vine. Keep abiding in Christ.

THE CHURCH AS A PRIESTHOOD

....

The church is a gathering of individual Christians into a special community of faith. Each and every believer is a part of Christ's church, and every believer has the distinct privilege of going directly to God through Jesus Christ. The fact that we can each approach God directly, rather than through some human go-between, is called the doctrine of the priesthood of the believer.

In Old Testament times, the nation of Israel had a high priest who represented the nation before God. In addition, there were many priests who carried out the work of representing individuals to God through the Temple rituals. That ancient priesthood was a high privilege and was limited to certain individuals.

In the New Testament we discover that God now looks at every believer in Jesus Christ as a priest. First Peter 2:5 says that God has made us to be *"a holy priesthood, offering spiritual sacrifices acceptable to God through Jesus Christ."* Then in verse 9 Peter writes, *"But you are a chosen people, a royal priesthood, a holy nation, a people belonging to God, that you may declare the praises of him who called you out of darkness into his wonderful light."* When we accept Jesus Christ into our lives, we immediately become priests in God's sight.

Like the priests of ancient times, we, as believer-priests, can enter into the very presence of God. We can offer sacrifices—not animal sacrifices, but sacrifices of time, talent, resources, and praise. Romans 12:1 says to *"offer your bodies as living sacrifices, holy and pleasing to God—this is your spiritual act of worship."* In addition to offering sacrifices, we can intercede for others through prayer. We have the distinct privilege of access to Almighty God! Hebrews 4:16 invites us to take advantage of our priestly privilege, saying, *"Let us then approach the throne of grace with confidence, so that we may receive mercy and find grace to help us in our time of need."* As believer-priests, we can enter God's presence at any moment through prayer.

As individual priests, together we form a single priesthood called the church. We serve under our Great High Priest, Jesus Christ. Hebrews 4:14-15 tells us, *"Therefore, since we have a great high priest who has gone through the heavens, Jesus the Son of God, let us hold firmly to the faith we profess. For we do not have a high priest who is unable to sympathize with our weaknesses, but we have one who has been tempted in every way just as we are—yet was without sin."* Jesus is pure and holy. He resisted every temptation, offered Himself as the sacrifice for our sins, and grants us access to the Father in heaven. As priests serving under Jesus Christ, we have the amazing privilege of approaching God directly and confidently. As a priesthood—the church of Jesus Christ—we have the opportunity of representing God to the world around us. What a privilege it is to be a part of the church of Jesus Christ!

THE FUTURE

THE RAPTURE

• • • • • • • •

Some days you just want to get out of town! You know what I mean. The phone is ringing constantly. The kids need attention. Work responsibilities are mounting, as are the bills that need to be paid. Face it, once in a while the urge hits you to catch the next plane and get away from it all for a few days. Actually, there are times when life seems so overwhelming that the only remedy we can imagine is the return of Jesus Christ. It's in those moments that we do take comfort in knowing that Jesus is coming again.

In John 14:1-3 Jesus said, *"Don't let your hearts be troubled. Trust in God; trust also in me. In my Father's house are many rooms; if it were not so, I would have told you. I am going there to prepare a place for you. And if I go and prepare a place for you, I will come back and take you to be with me that you also may be where I am."*

As Christians, we look forward to the day when Jesus comes to take us to be with Him in heaven. In fact, Jesus said to think about His coming as a way to overcome a troubled heart.

The apostle Paul had the same idea in mind. He encouraged Christians to take comfort in the truth of Jesus' return. In 1 Thessalonians 4:16-17 Paul wrote, *"For the Lord himself will come down from heaven, with a loud command, with the voice of the archangel, and with the trumpet call of God, and the dead in Christ will rise first. After that, we who are still alive and are left will be caught up together with them in the clouds to meet the Lord in the air."* This future event is sometimes called the rapture, a term that means to "snatch away." At any moment Jesus could come and snatch us up to be with Him in heaven.

Although Christians sometimes debate the timing of the rapture, the fact of the rapture can give us great comfort. The difficulties that this life dishes out will one day be far behind us. We'll be caught up to heaven to be with Jesus forever

All this will happen so quickly that we won't have time to make any last minute adjustments to our lives. First Corinthians 15:51-52 tells us, *"Listen, I tell you a mystery: we will not all sleep, but we will all be changed— in a flash, in the twinkling of an eye, at the last trumpet. For the trumpet will sound, the dead will be raised imperishable, and we will be changed."*

While the fact of the rapture can give us comfort, it should also motivate us to examine our current lifestyle. Will we be embarrassed when Jesus comes for us, or are we walking in obedience to His will? Have we accepted Him as our Savior, or will we be left behind? Only you and God know the condition of your heart today. Because Jesus could come at any time means we must be ready all the time. Why not invite Jesus, who died and rose again, to be your personal Savior today? Why not give Him every corner of your heart, committing yourself to living a life fully dedicated to Him? Jesus is coming again. Let's be ready.

THE RESURRECTION

. . . .

Springtime is one of my favorite times of the year. All around us we see new life. Crocuses, tulips, and daffodils emerge from the cold, lifeless ground. Trees that have been dormant for months begin to sprout new, green buds. The barrenness of winter bursts forth with life. Life from death—that's a theme we find throughout the Bible. We call it "resurrection."

When we talk about the resurrection, our first thoughts likely turn to Jesus Christ. He rose from the grave. He became, as Paul says in 1 Corinthians 15:23, the *"firstfruits"* of the resurrection. Because Jesus rose from the dead, we can look forward to our own resurrection.

The future resurrection of our human bodies is a concept that's introduced in the Old Testament. In Job 19:26 this ancient patriarch declared by faith, *"After my skin has been destroyed, in my flesh I will see God."* Isaiah 26:19 predicts, *"Your dead will live; their bodies will rise. You who dwell in the dust, wake up and shout for joy."* The resurrection will bring joy to those who have placed their faith in God. However, the future resurrection will be a day of judgment for unbelievers. Daniel 12:2 tells us, *"Multitudes who sleep in the dust of the earth will awake: some to everlasting life, others to shame and everlasting contempt."* We need to be right with God today so that the resurrection will be a day of joy, not judgment.

Three-Minute Theology

Jesus expressed this same thought in John 5:28, saying, *"A time is coming when all who are in their graves will hear his voice and come out—those who have done good will rise to live, and those who have done evil will rise to be condemned."*

For those who've put their faith in Jesus Christ, the resurrection of the body is a source of hope and comfort. But what will our resurrection bodies be like? Paul illustrated the distinction between our present bodies and our resurrection bodies in terms of the difference between living in a tent and living in a palace. In 2 Corinthians 5:1 he wrote, *"Now we know that if the earthly tent we live in is destroyed, we have a building from God, an eternal house in heaven, not built by human hands."* Our resurrection bodies will be specially created by God for unending life in heaven. In Philippians 3:21 Paul said that Jesus will *"transform our lowly bodies so that they will be like his glorious body."* Our resurrection bodies will be free from pain, free from defects, and fully reflecting the glory of our Savior. In some miraculous way, Jesus will reinstate life to the dust that was our physical bodies on earth. He will reunite our souls with our bodies for an eternal springtime of life and joy. This is the confident hope of the Christian. After all, we serve a risen Savior. Why not welcome that Savior, Jesus Christ, into your life today?

THE SECOND COMING

....

Jesus is coming again. The concept of the second coming is a key doctrine in the Christian faith. We believe that Jesus is coming again.

The Old Testament described the coming of the Messiah in terms of both a suffering servant and a conquering king. Isaiah 53:3 tells us, *"He was despised and rejected by men, a man of sorrows, and familiar with suffering."* Verse 6 goes on to say, *"The Lord has laid on him the iniquity of us all."* The Messiah had to suffer for our sins. But the Messiah would also be a conquering king. Zechariah 14:4 says, *"On that day his feet will stand on the Mount of Olives,"* and verse 9 tells us, *"The Lord will be king over the whole earth."* The ancient Jews were puzzled by this two-fold description of the Messiah as both a suffering servant and a conquering king. Some even concluded that there would be two Messiahs.

However, we know that instead of two Messiahs, there is but one Messiah—Jesus Christ—who reveals Himself in two distinct comings. At His first coming, Jesus arrived as a humble baby who grew to become the suffering servant. He died on the cross for our sins. However, Jesus promised that after His resurrection and ascension into heaven, He would come again as the promised conquering king. In Matthew 24:30 Jesus said, *"They will see the Son of Man coming on the clouds of the sky, with power and great glory."* Jesus is coming again to reign as our conquering king. He will return to earth in order to set up His messianic kingdom.

What will the second coming of Jesus Christ be like? The New Testament reveals a number of details about Jesus' return. For example, we know that Jesus will return personally, not simply in some spiritual sense, in order to bring salvation. Hebrews 9:28 tells us, *"Christ was sacrificed once to take away the sins of many people; and he will appear a second time, not to bear sin, but to bring salvation to those who are waiting for him."* We also know that Jesus will return visibly, just as He said in Matthew 24:27: *"For as lightning that comes from the east is visible even in the west, so will be the coming of the Son of Man."* Furthermore, Jesus will arrive triumphantly. Revelation 19:16 says, *"On his robe and on his thigh he has this name written: King of kings and Lord of lords."* Jesus is the King of kings and Lord of lords, sovereign over all creation. He is coming again as a conquering king. When Jesus returns, He'll bring salvation to those who have put their faith in Him, but judgment to all who have rejected Him.

Have you accepted Jesus as your Savior? We know that Jesus is coming again. Why not be prepared for His return? Invite Jesus to be your Savior today, and begin living faithfully for this King of kings and Lord of lords.

JUDGMENT DAY

· · · · · · · ·

According to the Bible, when Jesus returns He will *"judge the quick and the dead,"* or in more modern language, He will *"judge the living and the dead."* Peter states this twice, once in Acts 10:42 and again in 1 Peter 4:5. Paul also uses the same phrase in 2 Timothy 4:1. It would appear that the future judgment of Christ was a consistent theme in the early church.

However, the theme of divine judgment doesn't play well in our contemporary culture. We tend to focus on the love of God and neglect His attribute of justice. After all, it's more comfortable to think about God as a gentle, forgiving, even naïve old man than as a stern and righteous judge. While the Bible does describe God as a loving father, it also warns us that God is a righteous judge. We will all stand before Him one day to hear His verdict about our lives. We sometimes refer to that event as the judgment day, but the Bible paints the picture of a series of judgments that began at the cross.

When Jesus was describing His impending crucifixion, He said in John 12:31, *"Now is the time for judgment on this world; now the prince of this world will be driven out."* Sin deserves—actually demands—divine judgment. When Jesus died on the cross, He paid the penalty for our sins. His payment was sufficient to satisfy God's holiness and justice. Therefore, when we enter into a relationship with God through faith in Jesus Christ, our sins have already been judged. We are righteous in God's sight.

Three-Minute Theology

Nevertheless, even Christians will eventually stand before Jesus Christ as our judge. Second Corinthians 5:10 tells us, *"We must all appear before the judgment seat of Christ, that each one may receive what is due him for the things done while in the body, whether good or bad."* The judgment seat of Christ will not determine our eternal destiny, but it will determine our eternal rewards. Our destiny with God in heaven is assured when we put our faith in Jesus Christ. Our works, which don't contribute to our salvation, will however be weighed by God as He rewards us in heaven with various crowns—possibly a reference to levels of responsibility in His eternal kingdom. Therefore, we must serve God faithfully.

There is another future judgment described in the Bible, a dire day of judgment when unbelievers will forever be assigned to their eternal destiny in hell. Second Thessalonians 1:8-9 warns, *"He will punish those who do not know God and do not obey the gospel of our Lord Jesus. They will be punished with everlasting destruction and shut out from the presence of the Lord and from the majesty of his power."* All who fail to put their faith in Jesus Christ in this life will be separated from God forever in the next life.

Why not put your faith in Jesus Christ today? Then, and only then, will the day of God's judgment be a day of blessing instead of sorrow.

THE MILLENNIAL KINGDOM

. . . .

Every four years Americans vote for the highest position of leadership in our country, the President of the United States. Each candidate for that office promises a brighter future. We vote for—or sometimes against—certain candidates depending on our level of confidence that a particular candidate will make our way of life better. But we all recognize that there are no perfect candidates, and there is no perfect government. Deep inside, we long for a leader who can truly bring peace on earth.

Thankfully, such a leader is found in the person of our Savior, Jesus Christ. At His first coming, Jesus provided redemption. He died for our sins. At His second coming Jesus will bring righteousness to the world. He will rule and reign as the perfect *"King of kings and Lord of lords"* as Revelation 19:16 so aptly puts it. Jesus' future earthly reign is sometimes called the Millennium because, according to Revelation 20:4, Jesus will reign for *"a thousand years."*

The Messiah's righteous reign on earth is a consistent theme in the Old Testament. In 2 Samuel 7:16 God promised King David an eternal kingdom, saying, *"Your house and your kingdom will endure forever before me; your throne will be established forever."* As the ultimate descendant of David, Jesus alone can fulfill this promise.

The prophet Isaiah predicted that the millennial kingdom will be characterized by righteousness and peace. Isaiah 11:4 says, *"With righteousness he will judge the needy, with justice he will give decisions for the poor of the earth,"* and verse 6 tells us, *"The wolf will live with the lamb, the leopard will lie down with the goat, the calf and the lion and the yearling together; and a little child will lead them."* Not only will there be peace within nature, but there will also be unparalleled peace among the nations. Isaiah 2:4 says, *"They will beat their swords into plowshares and their spears into pruning hooks. Nation will not take up sword against nation, nor will they train for war anymore."* Truly the future millennial kingdom of Christ will be a glorious period in human existence.

When Jesus returns from heaven, He will establish this glorious millennial kingdom on earth. In Matthew 25:31 Jesus declared, *"When the Son of Man comes in his glory, and all the angels with him, he will sit on his throne in heavenly glory."* Jesus will reign over all the earth as our perfect, righteous, worthy King. At that time, as Revelation 11:15 says, *"The kingdom of the world has become the kingdom of our Lord and of his Christ, and he will reign for ever and ever."* That thousand year kingdom of Christ on earth will flow into His eternal reign over His creation.

Jesus Christ is our future King, but He wants to be Lord over your life today. Invite Jesus to be your Savior and your Lord. Grant Him the right to direct every aspect of your life.

HEAVEN, HELL, AND ETERNITY

....

When I plan a trip or a family vacation I need to know both where I'm going and how to get there. My desired destination will determine the route I take. When it comes to our eternal destination we want to be especially careful to choose the right path. Not all roads lead to heaven.

Jesus, in John 14:6, said, *"I am the way and the truth and the life. No one comes to the Father except through me."* The early church acknowledged this fundamental truth. In Acts 4:12 Peter declared, *"Salvation is found in no one else, for there is no other name under heaven given to men by which we must be saved."* The path to heaven is found only in the person and work of Jesus Christ. All other paths lead away from God and away from eternal life in heaven.

While our society doesn't like to talk about it, there is a real place called hell. The Bible describes this place of eternal judgment with a variety of images. Jesus used the burning garbage pit outside Jerusalem known as "Gehenna" to describe hell as a place of endless torment. In Mark 9:48 He said that in hell, *"Their worm does not die, and the fire is not quenched."* Hell will be a place of physical and mental agony. In Luke 16:23-24 Jesus used the term "Hades," which refers to an unseen place, a place of darkness, to describe eternal separation from God. In that unseen realm people are in *"torment"* and *"agony"* according to these verses. Revelation 20:15 describes hell as a lake of fire, warning, *"If anyone's name was not found written in the book of life, he was thrown into the lake of fire."* The Bible is clear. Hell is real. The only path that leads away from hell's eternal torment is Jesus Christ.

However, when you put your faith in Jesus Christ for your salvation, He rescues you from eternal punishment and guarantees your eternal bliss in His heavenly kingdom. Colossians 1:13 declares, *"He has rescued us from the dominion of darkness and brought us into the kingdom of the Son he loves."* We're already citizens of God's heavenly kingdom through faith in Jesus, and one day we'll enter heaven as God's dearly loved children.

The Bible describes heaven as *"the Father's house"* in John 14:1, *"a better country"* in Hebrews 11:16, and a *"holy city"* in Revelation 21:2. In that heavenly kingdom, according to Revelation 21:4, *"There will be no more death or mourning or crying or pain, for the old order of things has passed away."* The most impressive aspect of heaven, however, will be the very presence of our Savior, Jesus Christ.

Heaven is real. So is hell. Only one path leads to heaven, while all others lead to hell. Are you on the right path? Have you trusted Jesus for your salvation? Settle the matter today. Invite Jesus into your heart. Your eternal future depends on it.

Made in the USA
Columbia, SC
20 August 2020